Antidepressants

Other books in the History of Drugs series:

Amphetamines
Hallucinogens
Marijuana

THE HISTORY OF DRUGS

Antidepressants

EDITED BY WILLIAM DUDLEY

Bruce Glassman, *Vice President*
Bonnie Szumski, *Publisher*
Helen Cothran, *Managing Editor*

GREENHAVEN PRESS
An imprint of Thomson Gale, a part of The Thomson Corporation

THOMSON
GALE

Detroit • New York • San Francisco • San Diego • New Haven, Conn.
Waterville, Maine • London • Munich

THOMSON
✳
GALE

© 2005 Thomson Gale, a part of The Thomson Corporation.

Thomson and Star Logo are trademarks and Gale and Greenhaven Press are registered trademarks used herein under license.

For more information, contact
Greenhaven Press
27500 Drake Rd.
Farmington Hills, MI 48331-3535
Or you can visit our Internet site at http://www.gale.com

Cover credit: © Digital Image/The Museum of Modern Art/Licensed by SCALA

LIBRARY OF CONGRESS CATALOGING-IN-PUBLICATION DATA

Antidepressants / William Dudley, book editor.
   p. cm. — (The history of drugs)
  Includes bibliographical references and index.
  ISBN 0-7377-1951-6 (lib. : alk. paper)
   1. Antidepressants—History. I. Dudley, William. II. Series.
  RM332.A5733 2005
  615'.78—dc22
                                         2004052357

Printed in the United States of America

CONTENTS

FOREWORD 10

INTRODUCTION 13

CHAPTER ONE: EARLY DRUG TREATMENTS FOR DEPRESSION

1. TREATING DEPRESSION BEFORE THE TWENTIETH CENTURY 21
BY T.R. PAYK
Humans have a long history of using a variety of psychoactive drugs—including opium, alcohol, and hashish—to dispel feelings of depression.

2. THE DISCOVERY AND DEVELOPMENT OF THE FIRST MODERN ANTIDEPRESSANTS 25
BY ANDREW L. MORRISON
In the 1950s researchers noticed that drugs developed for various diseases coincidently improved the mental state of depressed patients. This discovery led to the introduction of the first modern antidepressant drugs.

3. A NEW WONDER DRUG FOR DEPRESSION 31
BY DONALD G. COOLEY
A 1957 article from *Better Homes and Gardens* praises Marsilid (iproniazid), one of the first antidepressants sold on the U.S. market.

4. WHY ANTIDEPRESSANTS WERE SLOW TO CATCH ON 36
BY CHARLES MEDAWAR
The slow spread of antidepressant use in the 1960s and 1970s may have been the result of doubts about their effectiveness and the fact that drug companies did not quickly focus on researching and developing them.

5. PROBLEMS WITH TRICYCLICS AND MAO INHIBITORS   42
BY PETER D. KRAMER
The antidepressants developed from the late 1950s
through the early 1980s often had serious and
unpleasant side effects.

CHAPTER TWO: PROZAC AND OTHER
ANTIDEPRESSANTS SWEEP THE NATION

1. A BRIEF HISTORY OF THE DEVELOPMENT
AND MARKETING OF PROZAC   51
BY EDWARD SHORTER
The popularity of tranquilizers and sedatives during
the 1950s and 1960s encouraged pharmaceutical
companies to develop other psychoactive drugs.
During the 1990s Prozac became the first popular
antidepressant nationwide.

2. A CRITICAL VIEW OF PROZAC'S FDA TESTING   63
BY STEPHEN BRAUN
Critics have accused Eli Lilly, the company that
developed Prozac, of manipulating clinical research
results in order to gain approval for the antidepressant from the Food and Drug Administration.

3. PROZAC—THE NEW WONDER DRUG   69
BY FRAN SCHUMER
Within two years of its introduction, Prozac was
being hailed as a miracle drug by many doctors and
patients.

4. A GRATEFUL PROZAC USER TALKS TO ITS CREATORS   83
BY TRACY THOMPSON
A newspaper reporter who uses Prozac to battle
her depression describes her experiences and those
of the scientists who discovered the drug.

5. THE PROZAC BACKLASH   90
BY DENISE GRADY
By 1990, reports of Prozac's dangerous possible
side effects filled the news, and the drug became
the target of lawsuits.

6. A WIDESPREAD CULTURE OF PROZAC USERS   103
BY NATHAN COBB
During the 1990s the widespread popularity of the
antidepressant Prozac affected cultural attitudes
toward drugs and depression as millions of Americans not only tried Prozac but openly discussed
their use of the drug.

7. PROZAC AND OTHER ANTIDEPRESSANTS HAVE CHANGED
THE PRACTICE OF PSYCHIATRY   110
BY SAMUEL H. BARONDES
The use of Prozac and related antidepressants revolutionized the practice of psychiatry and psychotherapy as patients eschewed talk therapy treatments in favor of drug regimens.

8. LOOKING BACK ON THE FIRST DECADE OF PROZAC AND
OTHER NEW ANTIDEPRESSANTS   116
BY NANCY WARTIK
Ten years after its introduction, Prozac has survived
controversies and criticisms and has had a lasting
impact on American attitudes toward depression
and drug treatment.

CHAPTER THREE: RECENT DEVELOPMENTS
AND CONTROVERSIES SURROUNDING
ANTIDEPRESSANTS

1. AMERICANS TURN TO NATURAL ANTIDEPRESSANTS   124
BY SOMLYNN RORIE
Many Americans wary of the side effects of anti-

depressants such as Prozac have turned to natural antidepressants, including herbs and amino acids.

2. ST. JOHN'S WORT IS NOT AN EFFECTIVE TREATMENT
   FOR SEVERE DEPRESSION   129
   BY DEBRA GOLDSCHMIDT
   The results of a large clinical study show that St.
   John's wort, a popular herbal supplement, does not
   help people suffering from major depression.

3. ANTIDEPRESSANTS CAUSE PEOPLE TO BE VIOLENT   133
   BY ROB WATERS
   Antidepressants have been blamed for provoking
   people to commit homicides and suicides; one
   noted case involved the wife of television comic
   actor Phil Hartman.

4. ANTIDEPRESSANTS MAY CAUSE TEEN SUICIDE   142
   BY MARILYN ELIAS
   The growing use of antidepressants among minors
   has raised concerns that the drugs may contribute
   to teen suicide.

5. DOCTORS BELIEVE DEPRESSION CAN BE CURED WITH
   ANTIDEPRESSANTS   148
   BY HARA MARANO
   Prozac and related antidepressants are a tool that
   some psychiatrists think may not only treat symptoms of depression but also cure the disease altogether.

6. MARKETING PAXIL AS A CURE FOR SHYNESS   155
   BY SHANKAR VEDANTAM
   The manufacturer of the antidepressant Paxil
   increased sales by promoting it as a cure for "social
   anxiety disorder"—a malady that many critics
   argue does not exist.

7. REPACKAGING PROZAC FOR WOMEN   162
BY MARGOT MAGOWAN
The manufacturer of Prozac is trying to boost sales
by marketing Serafem, a pill chemically identical to
Prozac, to women suffering from premenstrual
mood disorders.

8. THE NEXT WAVE OF ANTIDEPRESSANTS   166
BY MICHAEL C. MILLER
New research suggests that depression may be the
result of faulty nerve-cell connections that require
different kinds of antidepressants than those used
today.

APPENDIX

FACTS ABOUT ANTIDEPRESSANTS   169

TABLE OF ANTIDEPRESSANTS   171

CHRONOLOGY   172

ORGANIZATIONS TO CONTACT   175

FOR FURTHER RESEARCH   178

INDEX   183

FOREWORD

Drugs are chemical compounds that affect the functioning of the body and the mind. While the U.S. Food, Drug, and Cosmetic Act defines drugs as substances intended for use in the cure, mitigation, treatment, or prevention of disease, humans have long used drugs for recreational and religious purposes as well as for healing and medicinal purposes. Depending on context, then, the term *drug* provokes various reactions. In recent years, the widespread problem of substance abuse and addiction has often given the word *drug* a negative connotation. Nevertheless, drugs have made possible a revolution in the way modern doctors treat disease. The tension arising from the myriad ways drugs can be used is what makes their history so fascinating. Positioned at the intersection of science, anthropology, religion, therapy, sociology, and cultural studies, the history of drugs offers intriguing insights on medical discovery, cultural conflict, and the bright and dark sides of human innovation and experimentation.

Drugs are commonly grouped in three broad categories: over-the-counter drugs, prescription drugs, and illegal drugs. A historical examination of drugs, however, invites students and interested readers to observe the development of these categories and to see how arbitrary and changeable they can be. A particular drug's status is often the result of social and political forces that may not necessarily reflect its medicinal effects or its potential dangers. Marijuana, for example, is currently classified as an illegal Schedule I substance by the U.S. federal government, defining it as a drug with a high potential for abuse and no currently accepted medical use. Yet in 1850 it was included in the *U.S. Pharmacopoeia* as a medicine, and solutions and tinctures containing cannabis were frequently prescribed for relieving pain and inducing sleep. In the 1930s, after smokable marijuana had gained notoriety as a recreational intoxicant, the Federal Bureau of Narcotics launched a misinformation campaign against the drug, claiming that it commonly induced insanity and murderous violence. While today's medical experts no longer make such claims about marijuana, they continue to disagree about the drug's long-term effects and medicinal potential. Most interestingly, several states have passed medical marijuana initiatives, which allow seriously ill patients compassionate access to the drug under state law—although these patients can still be prosecuted for marijuana use under federal law. Marijuana's illegal status, then, is not as fixed or final as the federal government's current schedule might suggest. Examining marijuana from a historical perspective offers readers the chance to develop a more sophisticated and critically informed view of a controversial and politically charged subject. It also encourages students to learn about aspects of medicine, history, and culture that may receive scant attention in textbooks.

Each book in Greenhaven's The History of Drugs series chronicles a particular substance or group of related drugs—discussing the appearance and earliest use of the drug in initial chapters and more recent and contemporary controversies in later chapters. With the incorporation of both primary and secondary sources written by physicians, anthropologists, psychologists, historians, social analysts, and lawmakers, each anthology provides an engaging panoramic view of its subject. Selections include a variety of readings, including book excerpts, government documents, newspaper editorials, academic articles, and personal narratives. The editors of each volume aim to include accounts of notable incidents, ideas, subcultures, or individuals connected with the drug's history as well as perspectives on the effects, benefits, dangers, and legal status of the drug.

Every volume in the series includes an introductory essay that presents a broad overview of the drug in question. The annotated table of contents and comprehensive index help readers quickly locate material of interest. Each selection is prefaced by a summary of the article that also provides any necessary historical context and biographical information on the author. Several other research aids are also present, including excerpts of supplementary material, a time line of relevant historical events, the U.S. government's current drug schedule, a fact sheet detailing drug effects, and a bibliography of helpful sources.

The Greenhaven Press The History of Drugs series gives readers a unique and informative introduction to an often-ignored facet of scientific and cultural history. The contents of each anthology provide a valuable resource for general readers as well as for students interested in medicine, political science, philosophy, and social studies.

INTRODUCTION

An antidepressant, as its name suggests, is a drug used to relieve symptoms of depression. The term *depression*, when used to describe a person's state of mind, has at least two distinct meanings. It could refer simply to feelings of sadness, grief, anxiety, and loneliness that everyone feels from time to time. But the word is also a clinical term that refers to a serious mental illness that affects millions of Americans each year, with often disabling—or even fatal—results (depression is blamed for the majority of suicides).

If one uses the word *depression* to mean simply "feeling bad," then the list of drugs that could be considered antidepressants is long indeed. Virtually every mood-altering chemical people have taken throughout history, including marijuana, alcohol, opium, cocaine, and Ecstasy, could conceivably be considered an antidepressant if used to improve one's sense of well-being.[1] However, the term *antidepressant* is generally reserved for drugs specifically developed and prescribed to combat the mental disorder of clinical depression.

What Is Clinical Depression?

The clinical definition of depression refers to a category of mental illnesses called depressive disorders, which are characterized by sadness, difficulty in concentration and thinking, excessive fluctuations in sleeping and appetite, and in some cases suicidal tendencies. Author William Styron, who describes his own battle with depression in the book *Darkness Visible*, calls the disorder "a veritable howling tempest of the brain" and compares it to a storm that blows away a person's usual feelings and abilities to cope with life. Styron suffered from what is called unipolar major depressive disorder, or clinical depression, one of several different types of depression recognized by psychiatrists. A less severely disabling—but more chronic—type of depression is called dysthymic disorder. People with dysthymic disorder can still function in their daily lives, but can suffer from months and years of sadness and other depression symptoms. Another type of depression is bipolar disorder, also called manic-depressive illness, characterized by cycling moods of manic highs and depressive lows.[2]

Depression has been dubbed the common cold of mental health. According to the National Institute of Mental Health, in any given year more than 18 million Americans (about 9.5 percent of the population) suffer from a depressive illness. About 8 percent of people experience clinical depression at some point in their lives.

A History of Depression and Its Treatments

People have experienced symptoms of depression throughout human history, even though depression was not recognized as a disease. Accounts from Greece and Egypt four thousand years old describe people suffering from symptoms that would now be labeled as depression. People throughout history have often blamed the gods or spirits for depression and other mental disturbances; the sixteenth-century religious reformer Martin Luther, for example, blamed the devil for his bouts of depression. An alternative theory developed by Greek doctors and philosophers that became influential in Western civilization was that mental and physical health depended on a balance of the body's four "humors," or bodily fluids. The "humor" blamed for sadness was black bile, a substance that is secreted by the liver. In fact, the term *melancholia*, the Greek word that means black bile, was widely used in Europe in the seventeenth and eighteenth centuries to describe moodiness and other symptoms of depression.

Various treatments for depression have been tried over the centuries. Pierre Pomme, an eighteenth-century French physician, recommended chicken soup and cold baths for people suffering from the "vapours" (a condition with symptoms he described as "fatigue, pain, and a sense of dullness"). Bathing was a popular cure among the wealthy; by the nineteenth century many spa towns in Europe and the United States catered to people seeking a "water cure" for depression and anxiety; their hope was that drinking and bathing in water rich in minerals would bring them relief. However, in many cases little was done. People suffering from mild depression soldiered on in silence; those suffering from severe depression were placed in asylums or confined in their homes, where they could be placed on suicide watch but were offered little other treatment.

Various drugs and chemicals have been tried to help relieve the symptoms of depression. Since medieval times people in Europe have taken the herb St. John's wort for mental ailments including depression. People in China and Japan have taken ginkgo biloba for similar reasons. These and other herbs have become popular and have gained new scientific attention in recent times. In the United States at the beginning of the twentieth century, tonics and "patent medicines" were sold to people suffering from anxiety and depression; these medicines often contained alcohol or drugs that are now illegal or restricted, such as cocaine, opium, morphine, and heroin.

The first half of the twentieth century witnessed a decline in the United States in the use of drugs for depression. This development had several causes. One was the development of federal laws to ban and regulate drugs and medicines. The 1906 Pure Food and Drug Act requires that all products sold as medicines have clearly labeled ingredients. This act put an end to manufacturers slipping cocaine and opium and other drugs to an unwary public. Later laws made these drugs illegal to possess or distribute without a doctor's prescription. Other federal laws mandate that drug manufacturers prove to the satisfaction of the Food and Drug Administration (FDA) that their products are safe and effective for the conditions they are supposed to treat. Thus before they could sell a drug for depression, the manufacturers had to submit clinical studies demonstrating that it was an effective treatment for depression and that it was safe—a hurdle that often takes years to clear. The use of drugs to treat depression also declined in the first half of the twentieth century because the medical establishment was pursuing different treatments. The work of Sigmund Freud transformed how depression was treated, especially in Europe and the United States. Freud hypothesized that suppressed childhood memories create depression later in life. Freud and those who followed his methods developed and used psychoanalysis, a therapy in which analysts help patients recognize and gain power over their childhood memories and unconscious desires. Psychoanalysis and other forms of "talk therapy" became the preferred method of treating depression during the first half of the twentieth century. For cases of severe depression in which talk therapy was ineffective, scientists developed electroconvulsive therapy (ECT)—the administering of electric shocks to the brain via electrodes attached to the head. By the 1950s ECT was being used on thousands of patients for severe depression and other mental disorders, including schizophrenia.

The First Wave of Modern Antidepressants

In the early 1950s researchers made a pharmacological breakthrough with the development of drugs that had dramatic effects on people with schizophrenia and bipolar disorder. This development encouraged scientists to research chemicals that might help with unipolar depression. In fact, the first effective antidepressants were discovered by accident. In the late 1950s a drug being researched for tuberculosis was found to raise the spirits of depressed patients. The drug—iproniazid—was the first of what came to be known as monoamine oxidase inhibitor (MAOI) drugs. Around the same time, researchers investigating drugs they hoped would help schizophrenic patients found that although the drugs were ineffective for schizophrenia, they were effective for depression. These drugs, known as tricyclics (named for their chemical structure) hit the U.S. market in the 1960s under such brand names as Tofranil and Elavil.

These early antidepressants helped patients by moderating negative feelings, countering suicidal thoughts, and increasing the effectiveness of psychotherapy. Despite their success with some patients, the use of tricyclics and MAOIs was limited by several factors. One was the drugs' side effects, which many patients found unpleasant. These included dry mouth, dizziness, constipation, weight gain, and sexual dysfunction. People taking MAOIs had to avoid certain kinds of foods as well as cold remedies and other over-the-counter medicines because their interaction with the drugs caused spikes in blood pressure and other serious complications. Tricyclics, meanwhile, could be fatal with a modest overdose, which meant that patients required the close supervision of a psychiatrist to regulate the doses.

One interesting aspect of the history of antidepressants is that even after they were certified safe and effective by the FDA and were being prescribed, scientists still could not say exactly how and why they work. One theory, dating back to the early 1960s, focuses on chemicals in the brain. Brain cells communicate with each other by releasing chemicals called neurotransmitters, which include serotonin and norepinephrine. Antidepressants change the levels of active neurotransmitters in the brain and have often been marketed as helping the brain recover from a "chemical imbalance." However, many scientists today argue that simply ascribing depression to a "chemical imbalance" of neurotransmitters is at best a partial and oversimplified explanation of how antidepressants and the brain work. They continue to pursue different theories of the chemical causes of depression and the actions of antidepressants.

The Prozac Era

The history of antidepressants underwent a significant turn with the introduction of fluoxetine—better known by its brand name Prozac—to the U.S. market in December 1987. Its success soon inspired other companies to introduce chemically similar antidepressants, including Paxil in 1992 and Zoloft in 1993. These antidepressants are called selective serotonin reuptake inhibitors (SSRIs) because they increase the level of serotonin in the brain by preventing its reabsorption.

The attraction of SSRIs was not that they are more effective than the previous generation of antidepressants, but that they have fewer side effects. Because they do not have the same risk of fatal overdose as the tricyclics, doctors felt more comfortable in prescribing SSRIs to their patients. The result was a pharmacological revolution. Prozac quickly became one of the most popular drugs in U.S. history. In 1995 almost 19 million prescriptions for Prozac were dispensed in the United States; worldwide sales that year totaled more than $2 billion. Antidepressants were prescribed to teens, children, and even pets.

Depression lost some of its social stigma and aura of secrecy as Prozac and similar drugs became the subject of magazine cover stories and best-selling books. More people talked openly about their own experiences with depression. "With the success of the new SSRIs in treating depression, depression itself began to change," wrote medical historian Edward Shorter in 1998. "Once it had been an unusual condition that often led to hospititalization or even suicide; by the early 1990s the definition of depression had been greatly expanded to include a range of disorders that responded to new drugs like Prozac, and it was transformed into a common malady for which help is readily available."[3] Doctors also began to prescribe antidepressants for other mental illnesses such as anxiety and eating disorders.

The widespread sales success of Prozac and other antidepressants has not occurred without controversy. Some critics argue that Americans are rushing to antidepressants as a "miracle pill" answer to emotional problems that have social and spiritual causes. Other critics believe that antidepressants are not as safe or as effective as claimed, and many have criticized the process by which the FDA tests and approves drugs. SSRIs have been blamed for increasing thoughts of suicide or self-harm, sexual dysfunction, and long-term damage to the brain.

Future Trends

Despite the controversy they have caused, antidepressants appear to have a secure future. They have remained consistently popular, accounting for almost $20 billion in global sales in 2003. Whether the antidepressants most popular today will remain so thirty or more years into the future remains to be seen. Scientists continue to research how the brain works and to develop new antidepressants, trying to find ones that work with even fewer side effects. At the same time, many researchers are pursuing a different avenue by looking more closely at herbs, such as St. John's wort, that have been used for centuries to treat mood disorders. They are attempting to pinpoint and isolate the chemicals in these herbs that have antidepressant properties so that they can create even more powerful antidepressants. Regardless of which antidepressants fall out of favor and which emerge as the new Prozac, antidepressants are poised to remain the predominant treatment of depression in the twenty-first century.

Notes

1. Certain drugs, including alcohol, barbiturates, and tranquilizers, are sometimes classified as "depressants" because they act to slow down the activities of the central nervous system; *depressant* and *antidepressant* are not antonyms.
2. Only about 1 percent of people with depressive disorder have bipolar disorder. In 1949 lithium was discovered to be highly effective in regulating mood swings and has since been widely used to treat bipolar patients. The readings in this volume focus on drugs for unipolar depression.
3. Edward Shorter, "How Prozac Slew Freud," *American Heritage*, September 1998.

CHAPTER ONE

Early Drug Treatments for Depression

Treating Depression Before the Twentieth Century

T.R. Payk

For thousands of years humans have used drugs derived from plant extracts to dispel feelings of melancholy and depression. The following excerpt from an article by German medical scholar T.R. Payk presents a brief history of the kinds of drugs and therapies that have been used to treat depression. Opium, derived from poppies, was used by ancient civilizations more than four thousand years ago. Other drugs mentioned in Payk's historical survey include St. John's wort, alcohol, and hashish. In the nineteenth century synthetic psychoactive drugs such as codeine were first produced. This development helped pave the way for the later creation of modern synthetic antidepressants in the mid–twentieth century.

Depression has always counted among the most common psychiatric disorders, and today, the treatment of depression is one of the prime objectives of psychiatric therapy. A brief review of the history of psychiatry illustrates just how long attempts have been made to counter depression both with drugs and by other means.

The opium poppy (*Papaver somniferum*), a drug that enhanced well-being, was already known as the "Plant of Joy" to the Sumerians in the 3rd millennium B.C.

Opium, the latex from unripe poppy capsules, was also common in Minoan culture; during the Bronze Age in the 3rd and 2nd millennium B.C., it was a widely traded commodity. Until modern times, opium was used as an antidepressant in the form of "tinctura opii," prescribed in various dosages. *Atropa belladonna*, from the deadly nightshade, which has calming effects and stabilizes the autonomic nervous system in small doses, finds mention in the *Assyrian Herbal*, a formulation stemming from the 3rd millennium B.C., together with hashish. The ancient Egyptian kingdoms also knew of the psychotropic alkaloids hyoscyamine (from henbane) and scopolamine (from thorn apple), as well as alcohol; the latter was venerated as a remedy for melancholy in the Eber Papyrus dated 1600 B.C. It was used in this capacity until the first half of this century, and has probably remained the most commonly used, and abused, psychotropic substance.

Ancient Egyptian and Greek medicine also practiced playing music, dancing, and acting as forms of therapy in addition to the cathartic function of sleeping in temples. Pythagorean physicians, such as Alemaeon of Croton (around 570–500 B.C.) and Hippocrates (460–377 B.C.), declared insanity to be a disturbance of somatic function as part of their tenet of humoral pathology; their compendium of remedies included approximately 250 drugs.

In the late Hippocratic schools, medicamental therapy underwent vigorous expansion. In particular, phytotherapeutic polypragmasy developed; for example, not only extracts from poppy and mandrake were used to treat melancholy, but ass' milk and barley gruel were also recommended. The euphoric effect of hypericum oil was also applied for the treatment of depression. Although late Greek and Roman medical teaching was somatically oriented, it did also include psychological therapies such as music, entertainment, work, and distraction, as well as physiotherapy with baths, massage, and gymnastics.

The medical art embodied by Asclepiades (124–56 B.C.) and, above all, Galen (129–199 A.D.) gradually faded during the Middle Ages. Although the early Christian monasteries and communities still considered care of the emotionally disturbed a special Christian duty, medieval medicine inexorably sank into magic, mysticism, and alchemy. At the same time, during the 14th century, hospices for the insane were founded, so-called "madhouses," which more resembled dungeons than hospitals. One of the first to be established was the grim and menacing Bedlam in London in 1377.

In contrast, Islamic religion and Greek medicine gradually merged and developed into the outstandingly humane and profoundly scientific Arabic medicine. As early as 765 A.D., an exemplary hospital for emotional and nervous disorders was established in Baghdad. This was followed by others in Damascus, Fez, and Cairo. Under the Arabic influence, the first modern psychiatric hospital on European soil was founded in Seville in 1409. The famous Arabic doctors, Rhazes (856–925) and Avicenna (980–1037), doggedly fought against superstition and charlatanism, and practiced modern psychiatric methods that included milieu therapy and psychogogic measures. For instance, attempts were made to cheer and encourage melancholic patients with readings, music, and sexual stimulation. Alcohol, caffeine, cannabis, and opium were administered as antidepressants.

Despite countless pharmacologic trials during modern times, represented by the towering medical figure of Paracelsus (1493–1541), during which time St. John's wort played a role as "arnica for the nerves," psychiatric care and treatment was ultimately completely abandoned until the onset of a reform movement in England, France, and Germany during the 20th century. It still took over 100 years for the chains used to manacle patients finally to be banned from the madhouses.

Advances in Pharmacotherapy During the 19th Century

There had been no genuine advances in pharmacologic treatment for hundreds of years. The most common substances were opium and alcohol, as well as extracts from thorn apple, henbane, and deadly nightshade. The anatomist and psychiatrist [Johann Christian] Reil (1759–1813), a friend of [the German writer] Goethe and publisher of various medical journals, who was the first to use the term "psychiatry," warned against the indiscriminate administration of drugs and, instead, emphasized the use of psychogogics, occupation, playing music, and acting in his therapeutic program, "Rhapsodies" on the application of emotional cures on "rain of the mind." The treatment of melancholy included pleasing physical stimuli such as heat, studying esthetic paintings, strolling, and swinging.

The increasing application of science in medicine, which began around the middle of the 19th century, also benefited psychiatry. In 1811, a chair of psychiatry was inaugurated in Leipzig. Based on his understanding of psychophysiology and pathology, [Wilhelm] Griesinger (1817–1868), who finally became Professor of psychiatry in Berlin, postulated the physical origins of psychiatric illnesses, which he attributed to disturbances of the brain; on the other hand, he also fully acknowledged that psychodynamic processes could cause such conditions.

Tangible advances were made in pharmacology. In 1826, bromide was introduced as a sedative and hypnotic agent, and codeine was first used in 1832. In 1869, chloral hydrate was administered as the first synthetic sedative in the Berlin Charite psychiatric clinic; paraldehyde was introduced in 1882. The barbiturates have been known since the turn of the century.

In parallel with these developments, suggestive psychotherapy gradually became established, followed by psychoanalysis in the early years of this century; and behavioral therapy based on the learning psychology and behaviorism of the 20th century.

The Discovery and Development of the First Modern Antidepressants

Andrew L. Morrison

The drugs now known as antidepressants were first discovered and prescribed for use in the 1950s. In the following excerpt from his book *The Antidepressant Sourcebook*, Andrew L. Morrison, a practicing psychiatrist and mental health advocate, describes how luck played a role in their discovery. Iproniazid, the first of what became known as the MAOI (monoamine oxidase inhibitor) class of antidepressants, was originally tested as a treatment for tuberculosis but was discovered by researchers to lift the spirits of depressed people. It was sold under the brand name Marsilid. Imipramine, the first of what became known as the tricyclic class of antidepressants, was originally researched as a cure for schizophrenia before being approved as a treatment for depression under the brand name Tofranil. Chemical variants of these two medicines were developed in the 1960s and 1970s, Morrison writes, and are still being used today.

The antidepressants are a group of prescription medicines used for the treatment of depression as well as other psychiatric and medical conditions. Man's attempts to treat these disorders date back thousands of years, when the first surgeons drilled holes in the skulls of their patients (who had no anesthesia!) in order to expel "the demons within." Over the centuries, other treatment regimens have included bloodletting, exorcism, voodoo, magic potions, dietary supplements, herbal elixirs, and other home remedies, but no treatment was proved to be truly effective until the latter half of the twentieth century. The legitimacy of the antidepressant medications has withstood the scrutiny of hundreds of rigorously controlled scientific studies, and it is further substantiated by the millions of people all over the world who have benefited from them.

How Antidepressants Got Their Start

How the antidepressants got their start is an interesting tale, similar to how other discoveries in the field of medicine occurred: from a combination of luck and keen observation. Remember, for example, Sir Alexander Fleming's observation of what happened after a bacterial culture in his laboratory was accidentally contaminated by a mold. This led to the discovery of penicillin and the explosion of research on the antibiotics. The story of the antidepressants is just as fascinating.

It all started in the 1950s. While researching a medicine, iproniazid, to treat tuberculosis, doctors noticed that some of the patients receiving this medicine experienced elevation of their mood (even though their tuberculosis didn't improve). Based on this astute observation, researchers changed course and began studying iproniazid as a possible treatment for depression. One road taken by researchers was to explore the interaction between iproniazid and a medicine called reserpine. Reserpine was used at that time to treat high blood pressure. The researchers were interested in it because one of its side effects was depression. Iproniazid, investigators discovered, reversed some of reserpine's effects, which confirmed the scientists' belief that they were onto something.

Also in the 1950s, a new medicine, imipramine, was being

studied as a possible treatment for psychosis. Thorazine had just been discovered to have astonishing antipsychotic effects in people with schizophrenia, and imipramine was chemically similar to Thorazine. As it turned out, imipramine did not help the psychotic symptoms of people with schizophrenia, but it was noted to have some antidepressant effects. As was occurring with iproniazid, imipramine research then changed its course, and shortly thereafter, the first antidepressants were introduced. In the late 1950s, iproniazid and imipramine were released in the United States under the brand names Marsilid and Tofranil.

Nerve Chemistry 101

Efforts to solve the mystery of exactly how the antidepressants work also make an interesting tale. But before we get into that, let's take a quick course in Nerve Chemistry 101. The most important thing to remember is that it takes a chemical reaction for a nerve impulse, traveling along one nerve, to fire off a second nerve. Unlike the chemical reactions created in high school chemistry labs, which seem to take forever and often make students late to their next class, these reactions occur almost instantaneously. The miraculousness of this speed is matched only by the phenomenally small space in which these reactions occur. This space, the gap between the two nerves, is called a synapse. For the last fifty years, antidepressant research has focused more on these chemical reactions in the synapse than on anything else.

The first nerve releases chemicals into the synapse, and these chemicals stimulate receptors on the second nerve, firing off the second nerve and thereby transmitting the neural (nerve) impulse. Because they *transmit* the *neural* impulse, these chemicals are called *neurotransmitters*. The word "neurotransmitter" may be the most important word to know in the field of antidepressant research. However, don't forget that the neurotransmitters stimulate *receptors* on the second nerve.

What happens at the receptor sites is now being investigated as much as the neurotransmitters themselves, so the word "receptor" is becoming equally important.

The Catecholamine Hypothesis

Now, back to the 1950s again. Scientists knew that reserpine lowered blood pressure via its action, in the circulatory system, on a class of chemicals called the catecholamines. Catecholamines, significantly, are also present in the brain. Perhaps, they theorized, it was reserpine's effect on the catecholamines in the *brain* that caused the side effect of depression. And since iproniazid could reverse the effect of reserpine, perhaps iproniazid's antidepressant effect was related to its effect on brain catecholamines. Early research results confirmed these suspicions: iproniazid did affect brain catecholamines, which, as it turned out, do function in the brain as neurotransmitters. Researchers also found another neurotransmitter—one called serotonin. But the early studies focused mainly on the catecholamines.

What became known as the catecholamine hypothesis postulated that the success of the antidepressants had something to do with their affecting (possibly increasing the level of) catecholamines in the synapse. Here is a simplified version of the theory: In a normal brain, without any antidepressant present, after the catecholamines do their job of stimulating the receptors in the synapse, a portion of the catecholamines is reabsorbed back into the first nerve again. This process is called reuptake. Additionally, another portion of the catecholamines is broken down by an enzyme—the first step in the journey to the kidneys and eventual elimination from the body. When an antidepressant is present, however, the reuptake and/or the breakdown process is inhibited, resulting in an increased level of catecholamines in the synapse.

Excitement grew as investigators conducted studies to test the hypothesis. Was there just a deficiency of neurotransmitters in the synapse in depressed people to begin with? Did the antidepressants then correct this deficiency, raising the neurotransmitters to a normal level, thereby "fixing" the depression? Unfortunately, this theory was too easy an answer and didn't pan out in reality. The results of the studies just didn't fit the hypothesis. In fact, as often happens in research, there were more questions raised than answers found. To this day, researchers are still unable to find a hypothesis that puts all the pieces of the puzzle together and explains everything. . . .

Tricyclics and MAOIs

Despite the huge amount of time, energy, and money that went into new antidepressant research in the 1990s, many of the older medicines still remain on the market today. Just as penicillin continues to be a dependable weapon in our arsenal of antibiotics, so does Tofranil continue to be a reliable weapon in our antidepressant arsenal. Though iproniazid is now off the market, a dozen or so other antidepressants were introduced in the 1960s and 1970s. They, like Tofranil, have withstood the test of time, and continue to be reliable and effective antidepressants. They are the "old faithful" antidepressants. . . .

Imipramine, the first tricyclic [a class of drug], was initially studied as a drug for the treatment of psychosis. The reason it was being studied in the first place was that its chemical structure was similar to another drug, Thorazine, which had just been discovered to have strikingly beneficial effects on people with schizophrenia. The backbone of this Thorazine molecule consisted of three intertwined circular structures called benzene rings, and scientists were frantically investigating other molecules that also had this three-ringed structure. Imipramine had such a structure. In the two decades after imipramine's antidepressant effects were discovered, researchers found several other molecules that had both antidepressant properties and three benzene rings. Imipramine and its three-ringed descendants constitute the tricyclic class. They are named after their chemical anatomy, not after their chemical activity. The MAOIs . . . , on the other hand, are named after their chemical activity, not their chemical structure. . . . MAOI is an abbreviation for "monoamine oxidase inhibitor." Remember how the effects of reserpine and iproniazid led investigators to study the catecholamines in the brain, and how a portion of the catecholamines are broken down by an enzyme? Iproniazid, studies showed, increased the level of catecholamines in the synapse by inhibiting the activity of this enzyme. This enzyme is called monoamine oxidase. Iproniazid thus became known as a monoamine oxidase inhibitor. Several other antidepressants have descended from iproniazid. They also inhibit this enzyme and are also called MAOIs.

A New Wonder Drug for Depression

Donald G. Cooley

The following selection is taken from a 1957 article in *Better Homes and Gardens* describing a new drug called Marsilid (the trade name for iproniazid), one of the first prescribed antidepressants. The author, Donald G. Cooley, was a medical writer and editor whose works include *Eat and Get Slim* and the *Better Homes and Gardens Family Medical Guide*. In this selection he touts the drug as a breakthrough in the treatment of mental illness and depression, as well as other ailments, and cites patients and doctors extolling the new medicine as a "psychic energizer." However, shortly after the publication of this article, Marsilid was withdrawn from the market after more than a hundred patients taking the drug developed liver problems.

A housewife who had been tired and gravely depressed became so energetic recently that her husband complained, "She tires me out." A 24-year-old man said, "I felt like 60, now I feel like 15. I can't get depressed any more even when I try. I get a zest out of such common things as drinking coffee, breathing fresh air."

Behind these transformations lies a new drug called Marsilid, described by Dr. Elmer L. Severinghaus, clinical research director of the company that developed it, as "a compound that makes depressed or inhibited people feel more cheerful and energetic." Marsilid is the opposite of the famous tranquilizers, which revolutionized the treatment of overexcited psychotics,

Donald G. Cooley, "The Drug That Awakens Energies," *Better Homes and Gardens*, October 1957, pp. 18, 20.

and it is the first compound to break through the melancholy barriers of seclusion in a new and specific way. It could be the forerunner of a long-needed class of compounds that may bring a new zest for living to thousands of depressed people.

Astonishing Results

The drug has already shown actions that astonish and puzzle physicians. Reports from a number of clinics have been quietly accumulating in medical journals. Naturally, Marsilid does not produce 100 percent results in every case. No drug does. But Marsilid has proved dramatically effective in a high percentage of cases and against a wide variety of ailments. Rheumatic arthritis patients, though not cured, feel better. People with stubborn bone infections get well. Emaciated patients gain weight because of a stimulated appetite. Those suffering from mysterious skin ailments show almost miraculous improvement.

Perhaps the most vivid evidence of Marsilid's effectiveness comes from the Rockland State Hospital, Orangeburg, New York, where several mental patients now can dress themselves, make their beds, brush their teeth, feed themselves, and attend to personal needs. Until a few months ago these institutionalized women had been deteriorating, for 10 or 20 years, into mindless human vegetables. Shock, drug, and other treatments failed to help them. Some of them used to lie on the floor for seemingly interminable hours, inert, mute, unreachable, completely out of the world. They were more helpless than a newborn baby, which at least cries for help when it is uncomfortable.

Return to a more human existence—marked by smiles, responsiveness, group participation, greater tidiness, better self-care, and refusal to be "pushed around" by other patients—occurred over a period of weeks while the women received daily doses of Marsilid. The drug awakened long-smothered energies in 12 of 17 "burned-out" psychotics described in a preliminary report by Drs. Nathan S. Kline, Harry P. Loomer, and John C. Saunders, all of Rockland State Hospital. Another study of 20 depressed and debilitated patients, reported by Dr. George E. Crane, of Montefiore Hospital, New York, notes that the drug produced a great increase in vitality, a feeling of well-being, and "almost unlimited" resistance to fatigue.

Not that the drug is visualized as a cure-all or an easy pill for everybody who is down in the dumps. The drug is potent, and requires careful supervision. What is enormously exciting to researchers is the fact that at long last a breakthrough against widespread depression and heartbreakingly resistant forms of mental illness is now in sight.

Doctor Kline and his group call the drugs "psychic energizers." Another descriptive term might be "resurgitive," suggesting the resurgence of vital forces that have been hampered by chemical antagonists of the body's own making. Marsilid seems to be a moderator and balancer of these chemical forces of life.

Missed Clues

Looking backward, it is obvious that a glaring clue was missed when the drug was introduced as a tuberculosis treatment in 1951. The chemical name of Marsilid is *iproniazid*, confusingly similar to a related drug, *isoniazid*, which is a potent anti-T.B. chemical. One of the most publicized incidents in medical history occurred when tuberculosis patients literally jumped out of their beds and danced jigs in hospital corridors. They had received iproniazid (Marsilid). Their restlessly excited feeling of well-being was caused by large doses of the drug necessary in tuberculosis treatment.

This was a plain hint that a potent new "psychic energizer" was at work. But overstimulation is bad for tuberculosis patients. Marsilid was soon abandoned. Its sister compound, isoniazid, proved to be, and still is, one of the most effective tuberculosis drugs. There seemed to be no other use for Marsilid, and in 1952 its manufacturer was about to discontinue it.

Meanwhile, several investigators noted that doses of Marsilid small enough to eliminate most side effects had remark-able effect on diseases other than tuberculosis of the lungs. One of these men was Dr. David Bosworth, of Seaview Hospi-tal, and chief of orthopedic services at St. Luke's Hospital, New York, who urged the pharmaceutical company to keep on mak-ing the drug. He had been getting good results in tuberculosis of the bone, notoriously difficult to treat. Doctor Bosworth has published 10 papers in medical journals, giving technical de-tails of a variety of cases.

One middle-aged man had a painful cancer of fibrous tissue of the hip. Marsilid in no way halted the progress or fatal end of the disease. But it did some remarkable things for the pa-tient. He was not aware of pain; he gained many pounds de-spite a debilitating disease; his appetite was enormous; and he kept cooking equipment at his bedside so he could fix himself a steak at 2 o'clock in the morning. A photograph two weeks before his death shows a hearty, smiling man who clearly is en-joying life with enormous gusto and no thought for the morrow.

A man had chronic osteomyelitis (a serious bone infection). The drug freed him of a chronic infection that he had carried for 45 years.

An emaciated woman who had most of her stomach re-moved was unable to push her weight above 90 pounds. While taking the drug she gained 20 pounds and has easily main-tained her weight.

A young woman had acute lupus erythematosus, a myste-rious systemic disease, often fatal, which reflects itself in ugly crusts, blotches, and lesions of the face. Her progress on the drug is dramatically shown in a series of photographs—clear-ing, clearing, until the final picture shows a buoyantly healthy young woman without a blemish on her face.

Pioneering studies of the drug in rheumatoid arthritis have been made by Dr. Arthur L. Scherbel, director of the depart-ment of rheumatic disease at Cleveland Clinic, Cleveland, Ohio. In general, arthritic patients begin to show improvement in three to ten days. First, in responsive patients, there is rejuvenated sense of well-being. Depressed patients begin to smile. Appetite improves. Activity increases. Many say "I feel as I did before I had arthritis." They still have it; joint conditions do not change very remarkably. It is as if the patients had disease without symptoms. They keep active, feel strong, and do not fall into depressed, immobilized states that make arthritis worse.

Wide Applications

How can a single chemical compound of fairly simple structure have such wide application? One key is great psychic stimulation which awakens energies, lessens fatigue, drives toward zestful activity with less awareness of aches and brooding worries. Yet something profound happens in the body, too. Marsilid is not a germ killer, like an antibiotic, yet somehow it can reduce fevers and speed healing of wounds without direct action against germs. Where older, well-known stimulants generally lessen appetite, increase blood pressure, Marsilid increases appetite and lowers blood pressure. There's a lot to be learned about this fantastic drug.

Marsilid is a simple-looking white tablet, taken orally, available only on medical prescription, for it is a potent drug that must be administered with great care and in correct dosage. Possible side effects of mild constipation, transient dizziness, or slowness of urination can usually be overcome by adjusting dosage. Long-term use of the drug has proved perfectly safe to date.

Why Antidepressants Were Slow to Catch On

Charles Medawar

The first drugs prescribed as antidepressants were introduced in the United States and other nations in the late 1950s. In the following selection Charles Medawar provides a brief history of how they were used to treat depression over the next three decades. He explains that antidepressants were at first rather cautiously welcomed both by the scientific and medical establishment and by pharmaceutical companies. Medical textbooks continued to promote the view that most depressed patients would recover on their own with time and therefore did not need drugs. Scientists continued to raise questions about how the new antidepressants worked and published some studies indicating that antidepressant pills did not work much better than placebos. Drug companies concentrated most of their research and marketing efforts on drugs for insomnia and anxiety rather than depression. However, Medawar also identifies some reasons why the use of antidepressants gradually became prevalent, including their relative cheapness and ease of use compared to other treatments, public revulsion at electroconvulsive therapy treatments for depression, a growing belief in the biological basis of depression, and drug promotion by pharmaceutical companies. Medawar is a British-based consumer activist and author of *Insult or Injury? An Enquiry into the Marketing and*

Charles Medawar, "The Antidepressant Web—Marketing Depression and Making Medicines Work," *International Journal of Risk & Safety in Medicine*, vol. 10, 1997. The author substantially developed his work on these issues. See *Medicines Out of Control? Antidepressants and the Conspiracy of Goodwill*. Amsterdam: Aksant Academic Press, 2004. Reproduced by permission of IOS Press and the author.

Advertising of British Food and Drug Products in the Third World. He is also a member of the World Health Organization Expert Advisory Panel on Drug Policies and Management.

By the end of the 1950s, four MAOIs [monoamine-oxidase inhibitors] were on the market. They were originally described as "psychic energisers" but count as the earliest drugs still designated and licensed for used as "antidepressants". The main tricyclics (once known as "psychostimulants"), such as imipramine, came on the market a year or two later; they were developed from work on antihistamines (classically recognised as anti-allergy drugs). . . .

In the 1960s, the lack of any defined, mass market for depression inevitably meant that pharmaceutical companies were reluctant to try to develop drugs for it. Nevertheless, they had begun to see opportunities. Early on, one of the pioneers in this field [Frank J. Ayd] published a small, helpful and hopeful volume, *Recognising the Depressed Patient* and "Merck Sharpe & Dohme bought 50,000 copies of it and distributed it not just to psychiatrists, but to family doctors and internists and so forth".[1]

In those early days, no one knew how common depression was: "There were no epidemiological studies worth a tinker's damn. In fact, epidemiology as we know it today in psychiatry didn't exist then." An important turning point came with the publication of a widely circulated estimate from the WHO [World Health Organization] that "at least one hundred million people in the world . . . suffer from depressive disorders amenable to treatment".

With these changes came new and different kinds of antidepressant drugs with confident claims of effectiveness, plus more defined ideas about what depression was and how antidepressants worked. Two trends accelerated the commitment to use drugs. One was the ascendancy of biological theories of depression over psychoanalytically-oriented views. . . .

The other factor was the decline in use of ECT [electroconvulsive therapy], but not so much because of the risks, nor because it was thought ineffective. Medical texts tend to attribute the decline of ECT to public resistance fuelled by misconceived portrayals, notably in the book and film *One Flew Over the Cuckoo's Nest*. However, the evidence that ECT treatment is sometimes poorly performed and high costs may have also played some part. In the US, a single ECT session is costed at £200–£500 (mainly the cost of anaesthesia) and a typical course of treatment might be 6–12 sessions over several weeks.

Though drugs were usually cheaper and more convenient to use, their use has always been limited by poor compliance and unwanted effects. Patients usually experienced uncomfortable rather than serious side effects, though there were also significant risks. For example, recognition of a potentially dangerous interaction between MAOIs and certain foods (eg cheese, yeast extracts) helped to promote the tricyclics, and later the tricyclics lost some ground to the "quadricyclics", newer drugs promoted as safer in overdose. Very severe depression carries some risk of suicide, and it has often and long been argued that the greatest risk lies in not treating depression at all.

A Cautious Welcome

The scientific medical literature of the 1960s suggests that the original antidepressants were given a rather cautious welcome, though this should be seen in the context of those times. In those days, the market was quite small and the buzz in the journals (advertisements too) was mainly about anxiety, stress and insomnia. This was a huge and growing market, but strictly reserved for the "tranquillisers", and notably the benzodiazepines. Drugs like Librium (chlordiazepoxide) and Valium (diazepam) dominated, from 1960 and for the next 30 years.

Nor did "depression" mean what it means today. Then, (endogenous) depression was exemplified by the mentally and physically immobilised patient, sitting with his head in his hands. This was well-recognised as a serious illness but it also carried quite a stigma; it was [as psychiatrist Nathan S. Kline wrote in 1964] "not fashionable to be depressed". At the same time, most cases of "depression" were thought self-limiting: until the 1980s, the great medical textbooks and most experts emphasised that up to 80% of all cases of depression would cure themselves. If the implication was that depression often needed no drug treatment, such views come close to heresy today:

> . . . depression is, on the whole, one of the psychiatric conditions with the best prognosis for eventual recovery with or without treatment. Most depressions are self-limited and the spontaneous or placebo-induced improvement rate is often high. For example, in a series of nine controlled studies on hospitalised patients, 57% of the patients given placebo therapy showed improvement in two to six weeks.[2]

> In the treatment of depression one always has as an ally the fact that most depressions terminate in spontaneous remission. This means that in many cases regardless of what one does the patient eventually will begin to get better.[3]

> . . . most depressed patients get better anyway and the patients who improve after one has prescribed tablets have done so *post hoc* but not necessarily *proper hoc.* . . .[4]

Then as now it was recognised that a significant minority (around 25%) did not respond to drug treatment. The standard response to "resistant depression" today would be to increase the dose and to prescribe other drugs, as well or instead. In those days, resistant cases would usually be treated with electroconvulsive therapy (ECT); many experts believed this to be the most effective of all and some still do.

Less was known then about how antidepressant drugs worked and about the biochemical rationales for using them and, in those days, psychodynamic understandings of depression held much greater sway. Moreover, evidence had accumulated since the early 1960s of a gulf between the advertised benefits of antidepressants and their actual effects, when assessed in controlled clinical trials. As a whole, the hard evidence looked thin: it did suggest that the MAOIs and tricyclics could be distinguished from placebo, but the difference was not great. This was the rather low opinion of one of the pioneers [in 1964], a man [Jonathan O. Cole] still prominent in the field:

> The newer antidepressant drugs have now been used experimentally and clinically for approximately seven years. Their place in the physician's armamentarium is still far from clear, although many clinicians feel that the drugs are useful and effective. However, controlled clinical trials of these agents have not always led to unequivocally positive findings. Even when the findings have been favourable to the drugs under study, the differences between the efficacy of the drug and a placebo have not been as great as one might wish, or as one might have anticipated after reading published reports of uncontrolled trials.

Soon after [in 1969], the US National Institutes of Health reported the results of a systematic analysis of 490 studies published in 71 leading medical journals between 1955 and 1966. The conclusion was that: "the methodology of drug research is of more significance to the outcome of a clinical trial than is the drug being studied. . . . In well-designed studies, the differences between the effectiveness of antidepressant drugs and placebo are not impressive". The effect of these original antidepressants on depression has nevertheless become one of the main yardsticks for efficacy by which each successive generation of antidepressants has been proved.

Successive editions of a leading UK textbook on clinical pharmacology[5] suggest that the quality of such trials "has got only a little better since"; indeed, low standards seem commonplace today. Meanwhile, the number of tricyclic and related antidepressants proliferated, albeit to little effect. The 1970s and 1980s saw numerous attempts to manipulate drug molecules, but antidepressant drug therapy "developed a bewildering complexity" as a result. "None of these changes (has) produced an antidepressant that is more effective; approximately 80% of a heterogeneous population will respond to adequate treatment with any tricyclic compound",[6] and the same has proved true of the rest.

In time, the controversy quietened and antidepressant drug prescribing became routine, in spite of the uncertainties and probably because of them too. One factor which would have contributed to uncertainty was the complexity and cost of rigorous drug testing. Other factors would include the lack of evidently better alternatives; the lower cost and convenience of drug treatment; the "rewarding" and "gratifying" results sometimes obtained; growing belief in the biological basis of depression; the tendency to discount placebo . . . factors at work; confusion over the limitless opportunities for diagnoses, with possibilities for always trying something new; and perhaps above all, the intensity of drug promotion.

Notes

1. This quote and the one that follows is taken from a 1996 interview of Frank J. Ayd by David Healy, which appeared in the book *The Psychopharmacologists* (London: Chapman Hall [Altman], 1996).

2. Jonathan O. Cole, *Journal of the American Medical Association*, vol. 190, no. 5, November 2, 1964, pp. 124–31.

3. Nathan S. Kline, *Journal of the American Medical Association*, vol. 190, no. 8, November 23, 1964, pp. 122–30.

4. P. Leyburn, *Lancet*, November 25, 1967, pp. 1,135–38.

5. D.R. Laurence et al., *Clinical Pharmacology*. Churchill Livingstone, 1966, 1974, 1980, and 1987 editions.

6. From B. Blackwell and J.S. Simon in *Meylers Side Effects of Drugs*, 11th ed., Amsterdam: Elsevier, 1988.

Problems with Tricyclics and MAO Inhibitors

Peter D. Kramer

From the late 1950s to the late 1980s, most antidepressants fell within one of two general classes: MAO inhibitors and tricyclics. In the following selection Peter D. Kramer describes how these types of antidepressants were used in treating depression and the problems both patients and psychotherapists had with them. Many of these antidepressants had serious side effects, such as high blood pressure. In some instances the drugs caused fatalities. Researchers constantly sought to improve these drugs and create new ones with fewer side effects, he writes, but had little success until the introduction in the late 1980s of Prozac, the first of a new class of antidepressants. Kramer is a practicing psychiatrist and professor of psychiatry at Brown University. His 1993 book, *Listening to Prozac*, from which this selection is excerpted, became a best seller.

When Ronald Kuhn[1] chose to look at antihistamines as a source for antidepressants, he created a complication the field did not overcome until the advent of Prozac. The antihistamines known in the 1950s, as well as most developed there-

---

1. Swiss psychiatrist and pharmacologist who developed imipramine, the first of the "tricyclic" antidepressants, in the 1950s

---

after, tend pharmacologically to bring on the body's fight-or-flight response. They do this by interfering with a neurotransmitter called acetylcholine. When acetylcholine-related nerve transmission is diminished (as imipramine causes it to be), the body is ready for action. The heart beats rapidly, and energy is withdrawn from functions that can be postponed, like evacuation of bodily wastes. As a result, imipramine can cause a host of side effects—sweating, heart palpitations, dry mouth, constipation, and urinary retention among them.

MAOIs and Side Effects

Iproniazid and its relatives arouse the fight-or-flight response somewhat less often. This advantage alone might have made them popular. But an unexpected effect on blood pressure emerged in those drugs, a complication that pushed them to the sidelines, at least in the United States, and left the field to imipramine.

The drugs related to iproniazid are of particular interest because, although they are chemically quite distinct from Prozac, they can be seen, in terms of their effect on patients, as Prozac's predecessors. Like Prozac, they seem to reach aspects of depression that imipramine does not. In particular, it was recognized as early as the 1960s that they can be especially effective in patients who may not suffer classic depression but whose chronic vulnerability to depressed mood has a global effect on their personality.

The relatives of iproniazid are called monoamine-oxidase inhibitors, or MAOIs. Monoamine oxidase is the janitorial enzyme that oxidizes (burns, or inactivates) certain amines. By inhibiting monoamine oxidase, MAOIs prolong the effective life of those amines in the brain. In the years before Prozac was available,[2] a doctor might have considered putting a patient on an MAOI . . . but the doctor likely would have hesitated, be-

2. Prozac was approved for use in the United States in late 1987.

cause of concern over what else MAOI might do: in the 1960s, a rash of deaths from brain hemorrhage was reported among patients taking MAOIs; other patients, though they did not die, experienced severe headache on the basis of extremely high blood pressure, an odd occurrence because the MAOIs were used to *lower* blood pressure in people with hypertension. The means by which MAOIs make blood pressure skyrocket was elucidated in an interesting way. A British pharmacist who read a description of patients' headaches wrote a seemingly naïve letter noting that they resembled those his wife suffered when she consumed cheese, but not butter or milk. He asked whether the reaction might not be related to an interaction between MAOIs and some substance in cheese. Barry Blackwell, the doctor to whom the pharmacist had written, at first dismissed the suggestion—no drugs were known to interact with food substances in this way. But then he began to observe a series of patients on MAOIs who suffered headache and even extremely high blood pressure upon eating cheese.

Convinced that the "cheese reaction" was real, Blackwell set out to identify the offending ingredient. It turned out to be a chemical, ordinarily broken down by MAO, that causes nerve cells to release complex amines. Aged cheeses contain large amounts of this substance—so much that, when the janitorial enzyme is poisoned, a cheese eater on MAOIs will be flooded with biologically active amines, including ones that raise blood pressure.

Once the problem had been explained, it was a simple matter to advise patients to avoid foods that interact dangerously with MAOIs. But sticking to a restricted diet is constraining—the list of proscribed foods has grown over the years, and includes such disparate items as Chianti wine, fava beans, and ripe figs— and the requirement is dangerous for impulsive patients who "don't care if they live or die." MAOIs remained in widespread use in England, where they have been mainstay antidepressants for over thirty years. But in America the drugs were withdrawn from use, and even though they were later reintroduced, American doctors remained wary of them. Imipramine and related compounds dominated the medical treatment of depression.

Side Effects of Tricyclics

Imipramine, however, is a "dirty" drug—a drug that affects many systems at once. Not only are its side effects wide-ranging—the result of its action on nerves using such chemicals as histamine and acetylcholine—but imipramine's main effects are also nonspecific.

From the time antidepressants were developed, two different amines were understood to influence mood: *norepinephrine*, a substance that was familiar to pharmacologists because of its close relationship to adrenaline, and *serotonin*, another substance that is active throughout the body but about which less was known. Imipramine is "dirty" in its main effects and its side effects because it affects both norepinephrine and serotonin. Once imipramine's mechanism of action was understood, pharmacologists set out to synthesize a "clean" antidepressant—one as effective as imipramine but more specific in its action.

This goal proved unexpectedly elusive. In the three decades after imipramine's introduction [in 1958], pharmacologists synthesized and tested many chemicals similar to it in form. Like imipramine, the better known among these drugs, such as the antidepressants Elavil (amitriptyline) and Norpramin (desipramine), had three carbon rings in their chemical structure, and thus the group came to be called "tricyclics." Each new tricyclic antidepressant, as it was introduced, was said to have fewer side effects than imipramine—to have less effect on the acetylcholine or histamine pathways—or to act faster on depression. Some of these claims held up marginally. But most of the purported advantages evaporated as the drugs came into general use. None of the tricyclics is more effective than imipramine, probably none has a different time course of action, and all are "dirty" in the sense of influencing pathways involving both histamine and acetylcholine.

The only increase in specificity was the development of drugs that affected norepinephrine (and histamine and acetylcholine) without affecting serotonin. Desipramine, for example, is perhaps fifteen hundred times more active on norepinephrine than on serotonin pathways, and as a result a good deal of modern research has been done using this drug. But two goals eluded researchers: finding an antidepressant without side effects related to histamine and acetylcholine, and finding an antidepressant that preferentially affects serotonin.

This last goal was especially enticing. As the years passed, it seemed a number of conditions, ranging from atypical forms of depression to OCD [obsessive-compulsive disorder] and eating disorders, might involve derangements of serotonin. Here the MAOIs sometimes played a role. The MAOIs were very dirty. They affected not only norepinephrine and serotonin but a third amine, dopamine, the substance implicated in schizophrenia and Parkinson's disease. But the MAOIs were often more effective than the tricyclics for the disorders thought to be related to a lack of serotonin. Pharmacologists came to believe that the MAOIs' distinct efficacy might have to do with a strong effect on serotonin pathways, and that the tricyclics' limitations related to their lack of potency in raising serotonin levels. The new grail, pursued throughout the 1960s and 1970s and well into the 1980s, was a drug that would be like imipramine but that would selectively influence serotonin.

Looking for New Drugs

In its search for a clean analogue of imipramine and for an analogue that would strongly alter serotonin levels, psychopharmacology treaded water for over thirty years. This stalemate was frustrating to clinical psychiatrists. I remember as a medical student, and then again as a psychiatry resident, struggling to memorize charts regarding the characteristics of the tricyclic antidepressants. Generally, these charts would

THE HISTORY OF DRUGS

Treatment with Imipramine

Joshua Hadley, a writer and musician, describes his unsatisfactory experience with a imipramine, a tricyclic antidepressant.

I'd first tried an antidepressant—imipramine [brand names: Tofranil, Janimine; tricyclic antidepressant]—about ten years ago, when I was twenty-five. I felt stuck and depressed. I had a successful life by many standards: a good job, good pay, freedom to go where I wanted when I wanted. And yet I was floundering in emotional quicksand. I'd feel empty, then perhaps merely adequate, then empty again. In an apparently solid life was fluidity; in stability, nothing but unfulfilled expectations.

My psychotherapist referred me to a psychiatrist, who asked me why I was so depressed. I couldn't really say except that the world wasn't turning out as I'd expected. I left with a prescription for the imipramine. I took solace in the fact that it wasn't a dose for depression but for "anxiety." I recall hoping that the medication would save me. I quickly discovered that its main effects did not include salvation, but rather constipation, dry mouth, and difficulty in urinating, all of which made me feel worse. I tried to get used to the drug, but because of the side effects, I eventually said "Enough."

Joshua Hadley, in *Living with Prozac and Other Selective Serotonin Reuptake Inhibitors: Personal Accounts of Life on Antidepressants*. Ed. Debra Elfenbein. San Francisco: HarperSanFrancisco, 1995.

have a list of drugs running down the left-hand side and a list of neurotransmitters across the top. In each cell where the drug and a neurotransmitter intersected would be a series of plus or minus marks. Thus, a given drug would be + + + + for norepinephrine, + + for serotonin, – – for histamine, and – – – for acetylcholine. Medical students and residents for the most part do not mind this sort of chart; it makes demands on familiar skills and helps psychiatry seem like the rest of medicine. But the charts for antidepressants had no reliable relation to patients' responses.

The embarrassing truth about clinical work with antidepressants was that it was all art and no science. Various combinations of symptoms were said to be more serotonin- or norepinephrine-related, and various strategies were advanced for trying medications in logical order for particular sorts of patients. But these strategies varied from year to year, and even from one part of the country to another. It was true that a given patient might respond to one antidepressant after having failed to respond to another, but the doctor would have to manufacture a reason to explain why.

Psychiatrists were reduced to the expedient of choosing antidepressants on the basis of side effects. A patient whose depression was characterized by restlessness would be given a sedating antidepressant to be taken at night; a similar patient who complained of lack of energy would be given a stimulating antidepressant to be taken in the morning. But these choices said nothing about how the medications acted on depression: in all probability, both drugs amplified the effect of norepinephrine. It was as if, after discovering penicillin, researchers had synthesized a series of antibiotics, some of which incidentally made patients weary and some hyperalert—and then, when treating pneumonias, clinicians chose between these antibiotics not according to the susceptibilities of the infecting bacteria but according to whether the patient was agitated or prostrated by the illness.

Hopes that a more specific agent would make a difference were dampened by the advent of Desyrel (trazodone) in the early 1980s. Desyrel worked via serotonin, but its effects were difficult to distinguish from those of earlier antidepressants. Much of the problem, again, was side effects. Desyrel was so sedating that it had been marketed first in Europe as an antianxiety drug. You could do with Desyrel what you had been able to do with the tricyclics—treat a fair percentage of seriously depressed patients—but patients would tend to become tired or dizzy before you could get them on doses that radically changed the functioning of nerves that use serotonin. This was the stage onto which Prozac walked: thirty years of stasis. The tricyclic antidepressants were wonderful drugs, but in practical terms they were all more or less the same. And it was not clear whether a drug that was pharmacologically distinctive would be any different in clinical usage from the many antidepressants that were already available.

CHAPTER TWO

Prozac and Other Antidepressants Sweep the Nation

A Brief History of the Development and Marketing of Prozac

Edward Shorter

In the 1990s Prozac became a household word as millions of people were prescribed the drug for depression. In the following selection Edward Shorter provides a brief history of how Prozac was first developed in the corporate laboratories of Eli Lilly and Company in the early 1970s and eventually became a best-selling drug when it was introduced to the American public almost two decades later. Shorter suggests that Prozac served as a replacement for the tranquilizers and sedatives that were widely prescribed to Americans in the 1950s and 1960s but were later found to be highly addictive. The popularity of sedatives such as Valium taught drug manufacturers how potentially profitable the market for psychoactive medications could be, he writes, leading them to develop and then aggressively market Prozac and other antidepressants. Shorter is a medical historian and professor of history at the University of Toronto. He is the author of many books, including *A History of Psychiatry*, from which the following selection is excerpted.

Psychoactive drugs have always been available in one form or another to help people deal with depression and anxiety. Alcohol, which acts initially as a stimulant then a depressant, is as old as time. Opium achieved currency in the eighteenth cen-

Edward Shorter, *A History of Psychiatry*. New York: John Wiley & Sons, 1997. Copyright © 1997 by Edward Shorter. All rights reserved. This material is used by permission of John Wiley & Sons, Inc.

tury, and its alkaloids were used medically for depression in the nineteenth. The barbiturate sedatives had been available since the turn of our own century. Yet all had disadvantages in terms of addiction, daytime sedation, and inability to lift the core symptoms of psychiatric disorder.

The story of cosmetic psychopharmacology, the use of drugs with relatively few side effects to lift quotidian anxiety and depression, began with the advent of Miltown. Frank Berger, a Jewish refugee from Hitler, was the architect of this tale. Berger was born in Pilsen, Czechoslovakia, in 1913 and graduated in medicine from Prague in 1937. He fled to England and tossed about during the war as a bacteriologist, going to work in 1945 for the firm British Drug House. There he did some work with a muscle-relaxant called mephenesin, thinking that it might help patients with Parkinsonism. It did not, but Berger noted that it reduced anxiety for very short periods. . . .

In 1947, Berger immigrated to the States, becoming assistant professor of pediatrics at the University of Rochester, and consulting for a small drug house named Carter Products whose chief previous claim to fame had been "Carter's Little Liver Pills." Carter wanted Berger to develop a mephenesin-like product for anxiety, and the firm instructed their crackerjack organic chemist, Bernie Ludwig, to synthesize some new compounds. In May 1950, he produced one that was later given the generic name meprobamate. Yet Carter lost interest in the drug after polling a sample of physicians and asking them if they would use a drug that acted against anxiety. Most said no. Meanwhile, in 1949 Berger had joined Carter's subsidiary Wallace Laboratories in Wallace, New Jersey. Berger had confidence in meprobamate and, with his executive authority at Wallace, went through all the steps of working meprobamate up, arranging trials for a thousand patients, giving it to pregnant animals to see if it caused birth defects, even making a movie to show how meprobamate calmed Rhesus monkeys, who usually are very angry about being in captivity. Some people from Wyeth Laboratories saw the movie, expressed their interest to Berger, and learned that Carter Products wanted to sell the license. In 1955, Wallace began marketing meprobamate as "Miltown," Wyeth as "Equanil." Both names went on to have enormous resonance in American cultural history in the 1950s as "tranquilizers.". . .

In the following months, the demand for Miltown and Equanil was far greater than for any drug ever marketed in the United States. The supply in drugstores soon ran out and pharmacists would put signs in the window reading "out of Miltown" or "Miltown available tomorrow." Miltown became a household word when television-host Milton Berle started humorously referring to himself as "Miltown" Berle. The title of S.J. Perelman's 1957 book *The Road to Miltown* made the drug common coinage among the Book-of-the-Month set. *Look, Christian Century, Today's Health,* and *Time* ran stories about "Happy Pills," "Happiness Pills," "Peace of Mind Drugs," and "Happiness by Prescription." By 1956, one American in twenty was taking tranquilizers within a given month. Miltown was thus the first psychiatry drug to become the object of a popular frenzy.

Valium was the next frenzy. Competing pharmaceutical houses had been observing intently the emergence of chlorpromazine [a drug to treat schizophrenia] and Miltown. In 1954, Hoffmann–La Roche, a Swiss-based drug house with a large American office in Nutley, New Jersey, instructed its organic chemists to develop a "psychosedative drug."

Interestingly, neither university scientists nor government grants were involved in any of this: It was all driven by the profit motive. As Irvin Cohen, one of the psychiatrists who first tested Valium's sister-drug Librium later reflected, "The benzodiazepine [Valium etc.] story is essentially a model of how a therapeutic agent is conceived and brought forth by an enterprising pharmaceutical manufacturer who simply seeks to find a drug superior to others already in the marketplace." Thus Roche was merely hoping that its organic chemists would bring it abreast of the game.

One of Roche's chemists was a refugee named Leo Sternbach, who had received his PhD in organic chemistry in 1931 from Krakow's Jagiellonian University. . . . When Sternbach received this directive from on high in 1954, he thought about a class of dyes that he had worked with in Krakow in the mid-1930s. He set to work synthesizing a series of new dye-type products (benzheptoxdiazines) but got nowhere. All were inert in pharmacological testing on animals. Finally, the Roche management asked him to discontinue the research. In April 1957, as he was clearing his cluttered lab bench, he noticed that one of the compounds he had synthesized in 1955 had developed crystals at the bottom. With typical Central-European thoroughness, he decided to send it for testing, promising management that "this would be his last product of this series."

A few days later Sternbach got a phone call from Lowell Randall, Roche's director of pharmacology. This last compound in the series, later called chlordiazepoxide (Librium), had proven very interesting indeed. They were particularly impressed with its "taming effect" in a colony of imputedly vicious monkeys, at doses that did not otherwise affect the monkeys' alertness. . . . The drug did seem to have extraordinary qualities. Roche applied for a patent in May 1958.

In January 1959, Roche's medical director persuaded a few psychiatrists to try chlordiazepoxide on some of their office-practice patients. The patients did very well, becoming much less anxious and tense, and sleeping better. Emboldened by the enthusiasm of the psychiatrists, Roche marketed chlordiazepoxide in February 1960 under the trade name Librium. It was the first of the benzodiazepines, or "benzos," and during the 1960s was the number one prescription drug in the United States. Ultimately, there would be more than a thousand kinds of benzos on world markets.

Yet Librium had a number of side effects and could cause fits if suddenly discontinued. Roche felt the series Sternbach was working on had further potential. He was sent back to the lab bench. In 1959, he came up with a related benzo, diazepam, that was considerably more potent and that could be stabilized in pills. Roche marketed diazepam in 1963 as "Valium," which until the introduction of Prozac was the single most successful drug in pharmaceutical history. In 1969, Valium surpassed Librium as number one on the American drug list. By 1970, one woman in five and one man in thirteen was using "minor tranquilizers and sedatives," meaning mainly the benzos.

Impact on Psychiatry

The benzodiazepines had a dramatic impact on the practice of psychiatry. For the first time, psychiatrists were able to offer their patients a potent drug, unlike the mild Miltown, that did not sedate them. (The antipsychotics were simply too potent for routine use in psychiatry.) The share of psychiatric patients receiving prescriptions increased from a quarter of all office visits in 1975 to fully one-half by 1990 (from 25.3 percent to 50.2 percent). With the benzodiazepines as the entering wedge, psychiatry became increasingly a specialty oriented to the provision of medication. With the profession's main previous treatment modality, dynamic psychotherapy, now falling into disuse, an alternative lay at hand.

There was, however, one problem: The benzodiazepines turned out to be addictive, in the sense that patients' symptoms after trying to discontinue the drug were often worse than before starting. In recognition of their potential for abuse, in 1975 the Food and Drug Administration put the benzodiazepines and meprobamate on its "schedule IV," controlling refills and imposing on pharmacists special reporting requirements. Sales had already leveled off, and by 1980 Valium (diazepam) stood number 32 on the list of most commonly prescribed drugs, Librium (chlordiazepoxide) number 59. It was the end of "Valiumania." Nonetheless, the drugs had not exactly gone out of style: Almost 7 million prescriptions a year continued to be written in the United States for Valium-style products.

Until this point, there had been very little "unscientific" in the narrative. The benzodiazepines were perfectly appropriate for the treatment of anxiety and mild depression, and science-schooled psychiatrists did well to put their patients on them. Yet it had now become apparent that great sums were to be earned in the sale of psychiatry drugs. As Valium soared in popularity, awareness dawned among drugmakers that here lay the markets of the future. As the highly competitive drug companies rushed into psychopharmaceuticals, they began to distort psychiatry's own diagnostic sense. In trying to create for themselves market niches, drug companies would balloon illness categories. A given disorder might have been scarcely noticed until a drug company claimed to have a remedy for it, after which it became epidemic. As historian of psychopharmacology David Healy puts it, "As often happens in medicine, the availability of a treatment leads to an increase in recognition of the disorder that might benefit from that treatment.". . .

Against this background of psychiatric diagnosis increasingly manipulated by pharmaceutical companies arose the psychiatry drug that was to become the household word of the 1990s: Prozac. When Valium came along, both patients and their doctors were willing to define their problems in terms of anxiety once an effective drug existed for treating it. When Prozac, a drug for depression, arrived on the scene, the accent fell on depression as the hallmark of distress. "Our phone rings off the hook every time someone does a story about Prozac," said one physician at Manhattan's Beth Israel Medical Center. "People want to try it. If you tell them they're not depressed they say, 'Sure I am!'"

Developing Prozac

Prozac's pathway to fame began in July 1953 when John Gaddum, then at Edinburgh and one of the founders of psychopharmacology in Britain, speculated to a small but influential group of researchers, "It is possible that the 5-HT [serotonin] in our brains plays an essential part in keeping us sane." That utterance became the "signpost in the sky" of a whole generation of young psychopharmacologists. Gaddum himself had done some of the basic scientific work on assessing serotonin, and the early story was one of those triumphs of British pharmacology. But it followed that if serotonin kept us sane, increasing the availability of serotonin in the brain might counter psychiatric illness.

The scene shifted to the National Institutes of Health in Bethesda [Maryland], where researchers in Bernard Brodie's Laboratory of Chemical Pathology discovered in 1957 that an antipsychotic drug named reserpine could unlock the body's stores of serotonin. The Brodie group correlated behavioral changes with the presence of the various amines, and serotonin became a star. It was the Brodie lab, "LCP," that opened the whole psychiatric side of serotonin research. "LCP," recalled one researcher fondly, "was the Camelot of pharmacology."

But it's often forgotten that there was a British Camelot as well. The young researchers, inspired by Gaddum, were burrowing into brain chemistry at the same time as the Americans. In 1963, Alec Coppen, a biochemist-psychiatrist of the Medical Research Council and staff member at St. Ebba's Hospital, did a crucial experiment showing that serotonin-equivalents could relieve depression. Said Coppen later, "I claim this was the first observation that suggested that 5-HT [serotonin] was important in depression—an idea that is now the centre of a multi-billion pound drug market. But for many years, people said yah-boo sucks—there's nothing in this. Fashions are everything in medicine and 5-HT was not in fashion."

Coppen well knew. In the late 1960s, Arvid Carlsson had reinforced the news that serotonin seemed to control mood and drive. And Carlsson was coaching a Swedish drug company, Astra Pharmaceuticals, in its efforts to bring to market a drug that would inhibit the reuptake of serotonin in fighting depression. In 1981, Astra brought "Zelmid" (zimelidine) onto the market in several European countries. The experience ended in disaster: Two years later zimelidine was withdrawn from use as toxic. Nonetheless, Carlsson and Astra count as the initial pioneers of what would later be called SSRIs: selective serotonin reuptake inhibitors.

Eli Lilly's Research

One might easily bypass these tales of drug companies and their misadventures were they not such a key element in late-twentieth-century psychiatry. For at the Eli Lilly Company in Indianapolis as well, SSRIs were coming into fashion in the 1970s. The firm's senior pharmacologist Ray Fuller had been following international developments in serotonin. When Fuller came to Lilly in 1971, he tried to interest the firm in the idea that serotonin might have some action against depression in particular. Lilly was resistant. Recalled Alec Coppen of a conference at Lilly's base in Surrey in the early 1970s, "I'll always remember the Vice President of Research saying 'I thank Dr. Coppen for his contribution but I can tell you we won't be developing fluoxetine [Lilly's serotonin drug] as an antidepressant.'"

Yet Fuller, in alliance with Lilly biochemist David Wong, carried the day inside the company. Lilly organized a serotonin-depression team. In the meantime, Lilly had already asked chemist Bryan Molloy to synthesize a series of compounds that might function as antidepressants, minus the side effects of the tricyclics. Wong found that some of these compounds inhibited the reuptake of serotonin at the synapse, thus increasing its availability to the brain. (At present writing [in 1997], this concept is regarded as simplified: Antidepressants probably do not work by relieving a deficiency of a monoamine such as serotonin.) By 1974, lab tests were in progress on "Lilly 110140," which shortly received the generic name fluoxetine, later the trade name Prozac. In 1976, Lilly tested a Prozac analogue, nisoxetine, on healthy volunteers, who showed no side effects. The research also established that the drug did not seem to block the reuptake of other neurotransmitters such as noradrenaline, that it too, in other words, seemed to be a SSRI. (The acronym SSRI came into general use only in the early 1990s.) By 1978, Lilly was using the phrase specific serotonin reuptake inhibitor in connection with fluoxetine. Meanwhile, fluoxetine was being put into clinical trials in Indianapolis and Chicago: The results were promising although Lilly—perhaps for competitive reasons—did not publish them.

In 1980, the company decided to go all-out on the drug and sought some big-name biological psychiatrists to help test fluoxetine. John Feighner had . . . established his own private psychiatric clinic in La Mesa, California. Some very good news for the firm flowed from this clinic in 1983: Fluoxetine was just as good as the standard tricyclics in combating depression, and was without huge side effects. There was one more thing: Among the 12 different new antidepressants that Feighner was evaluating, fluoxetine was the only one that had as a "side effect" weight loss. (The first generation antidepressants often caused weight gains.) For millions of individuals, of course, weight loss is not a side effect but an ardently desired goal. A weight-reduction drug requiring no dietary restrictions would have an enormous market. After Lilly mentioned in its 1985 annual report that the company was developing a drug for weight loss, the stock soared.

Yet the more that Lilly tested fluoxetine as an antidepressant, the more the company put weight loss on the back burner, for the findings that came in from a number of field trials between 1984 and 1987 showed that patients would find fluoxetine much superior to the standard tricyclics because it had fewer side effects, making them feel, if anything, euphoric and "wired" rather than leaden and constipated. It also acted earlier and possessed a safer therapeutic window, meaning a wide margin between the therapeutic dose and the toxic dose (hence patients didn't have to be monitored with blood tests). In December 1987, the Food and Drug Administration approved Prozac for use.

In 1990, three years after Prozac was released, two re-searchers at McLean Hospital published an article suggesting that the drug was effective not merely for depression but for a range of disorders from panic to drop attacks ("cataplexy"). Since all of these conditions responded to Prozac (as well as to other drugs), they must have something in common, perhaps membership in an Affective Spectrum Disorder (ASD). This created an apparent scientific justification for expanding greatly the notion of depression, which now became one of "the most widespread diseases of mankind," as the authors put it. One of the authors, Harrison Pope, was quoted as say-ing that ASD affected "possibly one third of the population of the world." The prospects for Prozac became incalculable.

And so the word went out. By 1993, almost half of all vis-its to American psychiatrists were for mood disorders. Just as Valium had assuaged a nation beset by anxiety, the availabil-ity of a new drug for depression had produced a pattern of dis-order the drug was capable of treating.

Prozac's Wild Success

What followed was a media psychocircus of suggestion, as Prozac and its competitors were extended to the world public as a panacea for coping with life's problems even in the ab-sence of psychiatric illness (one recalls that the great majority of individuals with a formal psychiatric illness seek no treat-ment of any kind). Prozac is "much more than a fad," pro-claimed *Time* in 1993. "It is a medical breakthrough" that has brought relief to individuals such as "Susan," a self-described workaholic who becomes irritable around the time of her pe-riods and once threw her wedding ring at her husband. Now the edges of her personality had been planed off a bit. It would be ludicrous to argue that such people suffered a formal psy-chiatric illness in the historic tradition of the agonized and the inconsolable, for real psychiatric disease causes terrible pain and disablement. Yet here lay part of Prozac's core market.

Driven by the promise of problem-free personality and weight loss, Prozac took off more rapidly than any other psychiatric drug in history. By 1990, less than three years after its appearance, it had become the number one drug prescribed by psychiatrists. "With Millions Taking Prozac, A Legal Drug Culture Arises," headlined the New York Times. The black market that was developing for the drug seemed hardly necessary, for physicians were prescribing it for everything imaginable. "Prozac has attained the familiarity of Kleenex and the social status of spring water," said Newsweek in 1994. "The drug has shattered old stigmas," as Americans were said to be "swapping stories about it at dinner parties." By 1994, Prozac had become the number two best-selling drug in the world, following, perhaps ironically, an ulcer drug named Zantac.

Inserting Prozac into the history of psychiatry, requires untangling good science from scientism. Good science lay behind the discovery of fluoxetine as a much safer and quicker second-generation antidepressant than imipramine and the other tricyclics. . . . Scientism lay behind converting a whole host of human difficulties into the depression scale, and making all treatable with a wonder drug. This conversion was possible only because clinical psychiatry had enmeshed itself so massively in the corporate culture of the drug industry. The result was that a scientific discipline such as psychiatry nurtured a popular culture of pharmacological hedonism, as millions of people who otherwise did not have a psychiatric disorder craved the new compound because it lightened the burden of self-consciousness while making it possible for them to stay slim.

Yet the Prozac episode produced one massive benefit for the public good: It helped psychiatric conditions begin to seem acceptable in the eyes of the public, although we are still far from speaking of a complete destigmatization of mental illness. The "insane," who had transfixed the public view with horror for centuries, had now vanished to be replaced by people suffering from "stress" for whom help was easily available. Said Newsweek in 1990, a sure guide to the public pulse,

"As Prozac's success stories mount, so does the sense that depression and other mental disorders are just that—treatable illnesses, not failings of character." In the judgment of historian Healy, the pharmacotherapy of mild depression had evidenced itself to be so successful that one might conclude "'biological depression' is a mild illness for the most part and that those who end up being hospitalized for the disorder are an unrepresentative minority."

A Critical View of Prozac's FDA Testing

Stephen Braun

Before a drug can be legally prescribed in the United States, it needs to gain the approval of the Food and Drug Administration (FDA). Drug manufacturers often spend years funding clinical studies in order to gain approval for their products. The chemical fluoxetine (Prozac) was first developed in the early 1970s but was not approved by the FDA until December 1987 after years of testing. However, some critics have questioned whether the studies used to demonstrate Prozac's effectiveness and safety—and thus gain FDA approval—were adequate. In the following selection science writer Stephen Braun, citing the research of psychiatrist and drug critic Peter R. Breggin, describes how Eli Lilly and Company, the corporate developer of Prozac, conducted the testing of the drug. He concludes that Eli Lilly manipulated the results of its studies in order to gain FDA approval despite the fact that Prozac showed only modest success in its clinical trials. Braun is the author of *Buzz: The Science and Lore of Alcohol and Caffeine* and *The Science of Happiness*, from which this selection is taken. His work has also appeared in *Psychology Today*, *Science*, and other publications.

If there is a high priest of pharmacological Calvinism[1] it is psychiatrist Peter Breggin. Breggin believes passionately that all drugs for depression are bad, and he says that in his twenty-

1. the belief that people should not use psychoactive chemicals to feel good or alter one's consciousness

five years of practice, he has never started a patient on anti-depressants. He believes that depression is "obviously" a psy-chological and spiritual condition and thus he thinks drugs can never do anyone any good because they don't address the "real" causes of depression.

His extreme positions make him a fringe critic of "biological psychiatry"—though by virtue of his willingness to be branded a zealot or worse, his is the loudest voice shouting from the edge. Although his denial of a biological dimension to mental illness leaves him vulnerable to charges of irrationality, some of his points about the drug industry are cogent and important.

Breggin's fury with drug companies has motivated him to undertake some painstaking investigations that more even-handed critics would never bother with. And one of these in-vestigations produced findings well worth considering by any-one thinking about using the mind-altering products of the drug industry.

This particular investigation probed the way Eli Lilly con-ducted the testing required to get FDA [Food and Drug Admin-istration] approval of Prozac.

Because drug testing is inordinately expensive, and be-cause U.S. taxpayers don't want to pay for such testing them-selves, drug companies such as Lilly spend tens of millions of dollars to organize and conduct their own drug tests to pro-duce data to support their case before the FDA. The FDA is-sues many rules and regulations that attempt to control the way these tests—called clinical trials—are conducted, to min-imize manipulations that could make a drug appear more ef-fective than it really is. Unfortunately there are always loop-holes, and when a quarter-billion-dollar investment is on the line, those loopholes will be used to maximum advantage.

Breggin obtained FDA records and correspondence through the Freedom of Information Act and pieced together the fol-lowing story of Lilly's strenuous efforts to get Prozac approved by the FDA.

Three separate sets of clinical studies, or protocols, were

THE HISTORY OF DRUGS

A Critic Compares Prozac with Stimulants

One of the leading critics of Prozac in the 1990s was the psychiatrist and author Peter R. Breggin. In the following excerpt from his 1994 book Talking Back to Prozac, *he compares Prozac with stimulants such as amphetamines, arguing that both kinds of drugs are equally dangerous.*

A point-by-point summary of the comparisons between the classical stimulants and Prozac presents ominous parallels.

• Both groups of drugs produce stimulant syndromes in routine use.

• Both were quickly and widely embraced with testimonials by doctors and patients concerning near-miraculous mood-elevating effects.

• Both continue to be prescribed by many physicians who claim that patients experience few side effects and no withdrawal problems.

• Both reached epidemic proportions of prescription use.

• Both can produce very dangerous behavioral aberrations.

• Both are reuptake blockers that cause abnormal hyperactivity of serotonergic nerves and impact as well on the dopaminergic and adrenergic nerves.

• Both have repeatedly been whitewashed by their respective drug companies and the FDA.

The history of the pharmaceutical industry and the FDA in regard to amphetamines is telling. Physicians and much of the public know that stimulants are very dangerous drugs, yet the pharmaceutical industry and the FDA have been slow to mandate public warnings. The evidence is mounting regarding the potential of Prozac to cause many of the same devastating side effects—including violence and suicide—of the stimulants. One wonders how long it will take for the FDA or Eli Lilly to provide adequate warnings regarding Prozac.

Peter R. Breggin and Ginger Ross Breggin, *Talking Back to Prozac: What Doctors Won't Tell You About Today's Most Controversial Drug*. New York: St. Martin's, 1994.

used by the FDA to decide Prozac's fate.

The first protocol was conducted at six separate sites by six principal investigators—all chosen by Lilly. Each of these studies compared the effectiveness of Prozac against a dummy pill, or placebo, and one of the traditional antidepressants, Imipramine. In only one of the six studies did Prozac appear to be clearly better than the placebo on most of the variables tested—variables such as self-reported mood changes, improvements in sleep and eating patterns, increased motivation or energy, etc. The other five studies either showed Prozac to be no better than the placebo, or better only on a few variables studied (such as improved energy, feelings of guilt, and ability to concentrate). Most of the studies, in contrast, showed that Imipramine was clearly superior to the placebo in alleviating depressive thoughts and feelings.

To extract some lemonade from these lemons, Lilly used the fairly common statistical technique of pooling the data from the six individual studies. This technique has a subtle but extremely important effect: it makes it easier to prove statistical significance in differences measured among the groups. In other words, if Prozac improved a patient's self-rated mood by, say, 3 percent compared to the placebo group in a pool of only 15 patients, the result would not be considered statistically significant—it could be due to random chance. But that same 3 percent improvement in a pool of 150 patients *does* reach statistical significance, because, by the laws of statistics, in a larger group of people it is less likely that the difference would be due to chance alone.

The bottom line is that by pooling all six studies, Lilly magnified the neutral or only slightly positive results to achieve an effect it could claim was statistically significant. Again, the technique of pooling, in itself, is not unethical—in fact, it's fairly routine. But in this case the technique was applied to studies that, individually, only weakly supported the company's claims.

Unfortunately for Lilly, this technique still failed to impress the FDA. "Imipramine was clearly more effective than placebo, whereas fluoxetine [the generic name for Prozac] was less consistently better than placebo," the FDA wrote in March 1985.

Reworking the Numbers

Lilly reworked the numbers again. The company discarded the results of one of the largest negative studies. And they reincluded patients who, while they were in the Prozac trials, were also being given other psychotropic drugs. This tactic muddies the view of Prozac's effectiveness. When two or more drugs are taken simultaneously, it becomes impossible to know whether the Prozac was responsible for mood improvement or whether one of the other drugs was responsible. Despite this unavoidable ambiguity, the FDA accepted the protocol as evidence supporting Prozac's effectiveness.

The second of the three protocols did show Prozac as more effective than the placebo on most measures—though not on one of the more important ones: how patients themselves rated how they felt. On this measure, Prozac was no better than the placebo. Still, only 25 patients completed this protocol, and only 11 of these were actually given Prozac.

The third protocol used by the FDA as the basis for Prozac's approval was the largest, being conducted at ten separate sites. Two types of patients were studied: those who were either "mildly" or "moderately" depressed. In the study of mildly depressed patients, Prozac did no better than the placebo. But the group of 171 moderately depressed patients who completed the trial did show some improvement on Prozac, including their own self-report of how they felt. However, this protocol had some fairly serious design flaws, including a high dropout rate of participants due to unpleasant side effects such as agitation, insomnia, and headache (up to 50 percent in some groups) and the use of a "placebo washout"—a fairly standard but questionable technique in which patients who respond to a placebo in a trial phase of the study are dropped and the study is begun again.

This "weeding out" of placebo-responders may lower the overall placebo response in the "real" trial—which would be good for the drug company because the goal is to show that patients on the drug do significantly better than those on placebo. The FDA, although it allowed the protocol as evidence on Prozac's behalf, concluded that the study was "seriously flawed" and determined that "It is not possible to arrive at a single, unequivocal interpretation of the results."

It was on the basis of these studies that Prozac was approved for sale in the United States in December 1987.

Prozac's Effectiveness

None of this means that Prozac is useless for some people with depression. Far from it. . . . Prozac *can* be helpful—sometimes even life-saving. The point here is simply that Prozac is less of a miracle drug than most people think and placebos—sugar pills—are much *more* powerful than most people think. In addition, Eli Lilly's effort to win FDA approval for Prozac illustrates how powerfully drug companies are motivated to get such approval and how much effort must sometimes be expended in getting approval for a drug that has shown only modest success in clinical trials.

Prozac—the New Wonder Drug

Fran Schumer

The following selection is taken from a 1989 *New York* magazine article published about two years after Prozac was approved for use in the United States. The drug had already become celebrated as a treatment for depression and other mental disorders, including anxiety, bulimia, and obsessive-compulsiveness. Writer Fran Schumer describes several people who believe their lives have been changed for the better by Prozac. She writes that Prozac has advantages over earlier antidepressants, which had much more severe side effects. Schumer is a journalist who has also written for the *Charlotte Observer*, the *Boston Globe*, and the *New York Times*.

At 47, Alex,* a historian, assumed that he suffered from apathy, not depression. "All my life, I felt that everything was kind of a struggle. Everything was a little uphill. I really had to motivate myself to do anything. I was moody, easily irritated, and sometimes I didn't want to be around people." Now he's a changed man. He'll tell you it's the result of a drug called Prozac.

Less than two years after Eli Lilly and Company put it on the market [in December 1987], fluoxetine hydrochloride (its chemical name) is the antidepressant most widely prescribed by psychiatrists in the United States. When his doctor asked Alex to rank his feelings on a scale of 1 to 100 after several

---

Names and professions of patients have been changed.

months on Prozac, he said, "I've never felt this way before. It's over 100." He says, "It's been that way ever since."

A Big Success

Ten days after he put her on Prozac, Rachel's psychiatrist asked, "So what do you think?" "We should all go out and buy Eli Lilly stock," the 39-year-old investment banker said. "You're too late," he replied.

Even before Prozac was approved, the company's stock rose 7⅞ points in one day solely on the basis of reports that it might be useful as a weight-loss drug. And though the reports were overblown, sales continued to soar. From an estimated $130 million in 1988, they doubled during the first three quarters of 1989. Only a half-dozen drugs have sales of a billion dollars worldwide, and, according to analysts, Prozac is headed that way. "At this stage, no other antidepressant comes close," says Samuel D. Isaly, a partner at Mehta and Isaly, drug-industry analysts.

In this country, prescriptions of Prozac are soon expected to reach 1 million pieces of paper per month, all the more impressive given its stiff price—about $1.50 a capsule or, depending on the dose, anywhere from $50 to $200 a month. It's "terribly expensive," one user complains. But then, so is psychotherapy, and—some advocates would say—at least Prozac works.

Rachel's Story

When Rachel first started taking Prozac, she was skeptical. "I didn't expect it to do anything at all. I don't really approve of drugs. I had been on another antidepressant, and it didn't work. So I had concluded that drugs work only if you have a chemical imbalance, and I didn't think I did. I decided what I'd had was bad luck or a lousy mother, so I dismissed the idea that Prozac would work."

But a year ago, her boyfriend left her, got married, and had a child. A few years earlier, she would have gone out drinking with her buddies, but now they, too, were getting married and having children. Even Heidi of the *Chronicles* adopts a child, which is why Rachel refused to see the play. "I felt like the loneliest person in the Western Hemisphere," she says. Which still didn't seem like a reason to take drugs. "These things happen. How are you *supposed* to feel?" But even Rachel knew you weren't supposed to feel bad enough to contemplate suicide. She couldn't eat or sleep, and the tears were getting harder to control. "For some reason, the subway really did it," she says. "I'd cry every morning on the D train." Finally, after a particularly bad weekend, she told her psychologist she was desperate—"I'll try anything; give me heroin"—but she sent her to a psychiatrist who gave her Prozac instead.

Within days, Rachel felt better; within weeks, she was in a good mood. "Why are you so happy?" one friend inquired. "You look ten years younger—what did you do?" her 75-year-old bridge partner asked. "And then the most amazing thing happened," Rachel says. "I found myself humming little tunes at work. I'd walk down the hall humming something from *The Sound of Music*."

Like a lot of Prozac users, Rachel no longer dwells on the past—her mother or what happened in 1972 seems entirely beside the point. As for the present, "the facts of my life are exactly the same," she says. "I know that my career is some-place between a disaster and a joke. But instead of crying all the way to work every morning, I look at it as a puzzle. I still think I have no future as a heterosexual, and that used to make me so sad. Now I don't even think it's particularly a liability. It just doesn't matter. I never felt like that before. There's the sun in the morning and the moon at night, and the show looks beautiful in my backyard."

Her greatest fear, she says, is "that there will be a nuclear war and it'll interrupt my Prozac supply."

All drugs look like the answer at first. "The reputation of a new drug tends to follow a predictable course," instructs a paper circulated among psychologists and social workers. "First, there is unbridled enthusiasm; next, complete condemnation; finally, the drug takes an appropriate place in the pharmacological armamentarium after several years of open clinical experience."

Whether this will happen with Prozac is the subject of much debate. Skeptics point to Xanax, a Valium-type drug brought out [in 1981], unfortunately, can be hard to regulate and potentially habit-forming, though doctors still consider it an excellent drug. Then there was the far more serious case of Merital, taken off the market [in the 1980s] because it caused hemolytic anemias [a blood disorder] in some instances, and even fatalities.

But doctors doubt that this will be the case with Prozac. For one thing, it endured a lengthy period of premarket testing in this country and hasn't produced any mishaps abroad, where it has been on the market longer. "It's not really a new drug," says Andrew Levin, chief of the Behavioral Disorders Unit at Holliswood Hospital in Queens. "It's just new to the United States."

Not that Eli Lilly hasn't played Prozac to the hilt. Here and there in the offices of psychopharmacologists, scattered among paraphernalia from other drug companies, you see Prozac pens or Prozac clocks. In September, a group of physicians from one of the hospitals studying Prozac patients met at an Indonesian restaurant near the U.N. to discuss a study of the relative merits of Prozac. Lilly picked up the check.

Even so, reaction to Prozac in the medical community has been mixed, ranging from excitement to cautious optimism to a disdain for all the hype. "I think it's terrific," says Sandra Kopit Cohen, a psychiatrist and psychoanalyst, "but it's not a panacea." "It's a useful addition, but it by no means replaces anything," says Steven Roose, associate professor of clinical psychiatry at Columbia University. And in terms of its popularity, "the prescribing practices of doctors are often not the best indicator of what is good medicine," says Roose.

"It's definitely the drug of the moment in the antidepressant field," says David Hellerstein, physician in charge of psychiatric-outpatient services at Beth Israel Medical Center. "I think it's a marketing triumph; the question is, is it really better as a medication?"

Prozac and Other Antidepressants

There are lots of antidepressants, whole shopping carts full of mood drugs with eerily evocative names: Asendin, Desyrel, Elavil. The two main groups are the tricyclics and the so-called MAOIs (monoamine-oxidase inhibitors). Doctors like the tricyclics (Elavil is one; another is Tofranil) not only because they're effective (especially in cases of major, vegetative depression) but because they have been around for 30 years and are better understood. "It's not just enough to prescribe a drug," says Roose. "People metabolize drugs differently." In the three decades during which they've used the tricyclics, doctors have learned to measure the amount in a person's blood, thus raising the drugs' effectiveness rate, in optimal cases, from 60 to 85 percent. This means that despite the side effects that many patients experience—such as dry mouth, constipation, sluggishness, dizziness, and weight gain—"it's hard to find a new treatment that's more effective." (Roose does point out that tricyclics are also potentially lethal in overdose, a real danger with depressed patients.)

The second major group of antidepressants, the MAOIs (e.g., Nardil, Parnate), are considered even more effective by some doctors in what is called atypical depression (patients eat and sleep too much), and more of a nuisance too. This is largely because of the dietary restrictions they entail. A patient on an MAOI can't eat anything containing tyramine—pickles, pâté, tofu, caviar, herring, fava beans, yogurt, cheese, red wine, or beer. The restrictions notwithstanding, a user may still gain weight: Nardil is "the best pill ever made," says a former patient, except that she gained 70 pounds on it. Also, like tricyclics, MAOIs can interfere with orgasm. Nor has either group been effective in all cases.

Enter Prozac. It offers many advantages. It works in small doses (20 to 80 milligrams), it's fast (patients often feel the results in two to three weeks), and it's relatively easy to use. For these reasons, it's even more exciting to the general practitioner and internist than to the psychopharmacological elite. "For us, Prozac is a nice new addition to a sizable arsenal." says one psychopharmacologist. "However, for the local doc out in the country who doesn't know anything about MAOIs or tricyclics and is damned if he'd use them, Prozac is incredibly easy to prescribe. You can teach a chimpanzee to prescribe it."

For patients, the biggest advantage is the lack of side effects and restrictions. There isn't anything a person on Prozac can't eat, and all else being equal, he won't gain weight. In fact, in one study, patients on a leading tricyclic gained an average of three pounds while patients on Prozac lost three. But the real beauty of Prozac, fans agree, is that it doesn't usually induce a heavy, torpid state. "I get more of a medicated feeling taking antihistamines for hay fever," says one user. What another patient first noticed was the change in her looks. The perpetual line over her nose was gone—"It looked like I had had a face-lift," she says. A psychiatrist who has observed how Prozac works puts it this way: "It creates a sense of optimism and energy. You feel that it's worth making an effort; you don't feel hopeless anymore."

James, a 41-year-old lawyer, remembers exactly the moment he knew Prozac was working. "I was on vacation in South Dakota, on horseback in the wilderness in late August, and I had been taking Prozac for four or five weeks. I'm going down the trail and thinking about things, and I started to say to myself as I usually do, 'I wish I could change my life.' All of a sudden, I said, 'Why do I have to wish? Why don't I just do it?' That was the moment when I recognized the real change. Things didn't seem so hard anymore."

In the three months since, James has left his job to go back to an old one, realizing that his mood, not the original job, was the problem. He's less equivocal with his girlfriend. For the first time in his adult life, even marriage seems like a possibility. "It's not that I have the best day I've ever had every day," he explains, "but basically, I look forward to every one." During a particularly busy spell last summer, he paused mid-frenzy and thought, "God, I'm so efficient. I've never been able to handle this much work." In the past, "I'd be so anxious about doing something. I couldn't start. Now I just say, 'Okay, let's go.'"

Diagnosing Depression

It used to be a lot easier to know if you were depressed. Classical major depression meant that you couldn't eat and couldn't sleep, and that nothing could cheer you up. But recent studies suggest that depression is much more varied. There's atypical depression and major depression, but also dysthymia, a chronic, low-grade depression that in some ways is hard to distinguish from the plain old blues. "What we're talking about here is the walking wounded," says Camille Hemlock, a resident at Beth Israel Medical Center who is studying dysthymia, "people who always look at the glass as half-empty." And though, by this definition, many are quasi-dysthymic, pure dysthymia is a very particular disease. According to the *Diagnostic and Statistical Manual of Mental Disorders* of the American Psychiatric Association, a person is dysthymic if he or she is mildly depressed for a minimum of two years and displays at least two of these symptoms: poor appetite (or too much), insomnia or hypersomnia, low energy, low self-esteem, poor concentration, indecisiveness, and despair. As one dysthymic says, "I'd dread every single day."

About 3 or 4 of every 100 people suffer from dysthymia, which is more common in women, and apparently also in single people and the low-income young. And because it often leads to major depression and, in some cases, suicide, "it's recognized as a significant public-health problem," says Robert F.

Prien, head of the Treatment of Mood Disorders Research Program at the National Institute of Mental Health.

It wasn't so long ago that dysthymia was viewed as just your basic neurosis, for which people were shuffled into psychotherapy for years. But in the third edition of the *Diagnostic and Statistical Manual*, dysthymia made the leap from personality disorder to mood disorder. "Now it was categorized with conditions known to have biological origins," says Beth Israel's Dr. Hellerstein. And if the cause was biological, then, possibly, so was the treatment.

Studies using Prozac are in the works. One, at the New York State Psychiatric Institute, will eventually treat more than 400 patients, among them many dysthymics. . . . Another, at Beth Israel . . . is treating about 30 dysthymic patients with Prozac and trazodone. Though that study is far from complete, the results already look good. "Without question, there's a major role for Prozac in chronic depression," a senior researcher says.

"The fact is, we're all depressed. The whole world is depressed. I don't know a human being who isn't," says one doctor. Which raises the question, should everyone take Prozac?

If people do, the drug won't help unless they're biochemically depressed. "It's like aspirin," says Dr. Kopit Cohen. "If you don't have a headache, it doesn't work. It's not like cocaine or Valium. Everyone feels better on Valium."

The more radical question, says another psychiatrist, is whether everybody will be taking Prozac someday. It's unlikely. Professionally, antidepressant use isn't the most helpful admission to make on a job application, and on a personal level, not everyone approves. But the biggest problem with Prozac is that it isn't a cure. Take away the pill and those bad feelings return.

Moreover, Prozac doesn't work for everyone who tries it. Even its advocates agree that it's not the first choice in cases of severe depression, where a physician is more concerned with efficacy than ease of use. Moreover, Prozac can have its nasty side. "It was four months of crying every day," says a 50-year-old poet of her time on Prozac. Of 4,000 patients given the drug in clinical tests, 15 percent discontinued treatment because of adverse reactions—anxiety, insomnia, nausea, or stomach pain, and, in a smaller percentage of cases, headache, skin rash, or sexual dysfunction, particularly ejaculation problems. Although Eli Lilly estimates the incidence of sexual dysfunction at only 1.6 percent, "we tend to see it in more than 2 percent of our male patients," says Joel S. Hoffman, clinical assistant professor of psychiatry at Columbia University.

By far the most serious effect is the caffeine syndrome. In milder cases, Prozac users have trouble falling asleep. In more extreme ones, patients feel they want to crawl out of their skin. "We've all seen fairly severe agitation reactions," says Dr. Hoffman. "A physician I treated described his reaction to Prozac as the worst experience in his life. And this is not someone given to overstatement."

Which makes doctors somewhat restrained in their praise. "I think it's a terrific medication, but it's not that everyone either feels nothing or feels better," Hoffman says. "Some people feel worse." Nevertheless, they are outnumbered by born-again Prozac users. And because of the different and, in most cases, better-tolerated spectrum of side effects, the compliance rate with Prozac is high. "Other than one patient with a rash and one who had trouble tolerating it because of an upset stomach, I've had much less trouble and therefore much more acceptance of it," says George S. Bell, director of outpatient psychiatry at Albert Einstein Medical Center in Philadelphia.

Consequently, some patients are willing to go to any lengths to stay on Prozac. When she first linked her sharp stomach pains to Prozac, one user thought, "Well, what if it is the Prozac? Would I rather go back to feeling the way I felt before?" She decided she'd rather endure the stomach pains. Another says, "If all my hair fell out, I'd still take it." To those who object to taking any kind of antidepressant, Prozac users counter that they have a chemical imbalance that prevents them from putting *any* therapy to good use. "It's like trying to work therapy on someone with acute appendicitis," says Hoffman. "It hurts so much, it's hard to listen and work the therapy."

A Positive Pandora's Box

As an antidepressant, Prozac is one of dozens of possible drugs. But what also impresses physicians is the broad spectrum of disorders on which it works—severe ailments such as anxiety attacks, bulimia, and obsessive-compulsive disorders, and lesser ones like PMS and nicotine withdrawal. "Prozac and other antidepressants may open Pandora's box, but in a positive way," says David Hellerstein. Obsessive-compulsive disorders affect 1 to 3 percent of the population. "Even the most optimistic people are in agreement that psychoanalysis is not very effective on obsessive-compulsive disorders," Hellerstein says,

"Many of us were waiting for Prozac to come to this country, since it's as good a drug as is available for obsessive-compulsive disorders," Holliswood Hospital's Dr. Levin says. In one study, Prozac significantly reduced the symptoms in 60 percent of the obsessive-compulsive patients on whom it was tried, and some researchers push that figure to 80 percent.

Bernice, a 42-year-old mother of three, was so terrified of disease that she wouldn't keep cans in the house. And for fear of AIDS, she wouldn't work in her insurance office, visit friends, or eat in a restaurant where she might come into contact with homosexuals. After twelve weeks on Prozac, her symptoms were down to a "real minimum," her psychologist says. Now she stocks cans, eats out, visits friends.

The drug works for children too. Third-grader Janey worked as if she were an aspiring Rhodes scholar, checking and rechecking her homework, reading and rereading her notes. Sometimes she would wake at 3 A.M. to do it all again. Another of her obsessions was hair-pulling.

Her psychologist diagnosed her as suffering from an obsessive-compulsive disorder with agitated depressive symptoms and sent her to a psychiatrist. Within a month after she started Prozac, Janey's symptoms were substantially relieved. "It's much easier to think of prescribing Prozac for children because of the relative lack of side effects," says Michelle Gersten, assistant professor of child psychiatry at the Mount Sinai School of Medicine. "The dry mouth and constipation can be hard for children to endure; they're hard for adults. And giving adolescents pills on which they might gain weight?"

Prozac and Weight Loss

The myth surrounding Prozac as a weight-loss drug is largely just that—according to most doctors, any such effects are short-term—but its impact on people with eating disorders has been very heartening. One woman thought she was hypoglycemic until she took Prozac and found that her symptoms disappeared. "For the first time in my life, I don't care if I eat at 6 or 10 P.M.," she says. "I feel hungry like a normal person—my stomach does growl—but I don't feel that I'm growing fangs."

Another woman, a compulsive overeater, says that though Overeaters Anonymous arrested most of her compulsive eating symptoms, Prozac also helped. Now, she says, her desire to binge has decreased. "I still have my days, but nowhere like before I joined OA or even while I was in it." On Prozac, "I eat when I'm hungry and stop when I'm full."

Although MAOIs may be more effective for bulimia, experts recommend trying Prozac first because it's so easy to prescribe and use. And given the weight phobia of bulimic patients, the appeal is obvious. "With our patients, we say, 'Ethically, we're bound to tell you that one of the side effects of Prozac is that it causes weight loss in some people,'" says a physician who treats bulimics. "Their response is 'Where's the nearest drugstore?'"

Unfortunately, neither Prozac nor any other drug has been able to alleviate anorexia. "Something about being thin interferes with the way the drug works," says Harrison G. Pope, associate professor of psychiatry at Harvard Medical School and chief of the Biological Psychiatry Laboratory at McLean Hospital in Belmont, Massachusetts. But patients suffering from PMS and nicotine withdrawal do respond well, at least according to preliminary reports. In cases in which women with PMS were given Prozac for depression, many reported that their symptoms lifted or decreased. "In one case the change was quite dramatic," says Dr. Bell. "The patient had suffered significantly." A small pilot study of Prozac's anti-nicotine effects, conducted by William Hapworth, a Manhattan psychiatrist, and his psychologist wife, Mada, reports that after six months of taking the drug, 80 percent of the ex-smokers under observation were less irritable and experienced fewer cravings.

Despite its slightly agitating effect, Prozac has also been used to treat panic disorders. When 25 patients were given a quarter-capsule (5 milligrams) a day, "75 to 80 percent responded quite nicely," reports Michael R. Liebowitz, associate professor of clinical psychiatry at Columbia University and director of the Anxiety Disorders Clinic at the New York State Psychiatric Institute.

Future Risks

What remains to be seen is whether Prozac has side effects that haven't cropped up yet. Premarket tests typically involve 6,000 or 7,000 users. But Prozac's enormous popularity means that it is probably being used by millions. Consequently, "if there are going to be any surprises, they're going to come out," one psychiatrist says.

Not everyone cares. When asked if she thought she might have to take Prozac forever, one user replied, "I hope so." Lifelong depression requires lifelong treatment. There's a risk associated with not taking the medicine, as well. "Studies show that depressed people are more vulnerable to cancer, immune problems, and assorted other medical disorders," one psychiatrist says. In the meantime, there's been no smoking gun. "I usually get an update from the drug company of any bizarre adverse reactions, and though not everyone reports everything, there's been nothing outrageous," a senior researcher says. Given the number of people taking Prozac and the absence of problems so far, most physicians are impressed. "I'd be surprised if there were any surprises," a psychiatrist says.

Many therapists feel that their profession has been buoyed not only by advances in drug therapy but by the wider acceptance of the need for therapy combined with drugs. "Sophisticated people don't talk about either/or," says Columbia Presbyterian's Roose.

Prozac users acknowledge the continued need for therapy and often are more enthusiastic about it once they've started taking the drug. "Wonderful—I love it," one social worker says about her therapy now. "The Prozac has allowed me to achieve new levels of insight." Rather than negate her first twelve years in therapy, she says, "I've needed all the help I've gotten." Not everyone is so charitable. "I'm angry at my therapist because I mentioned Prozac more than once and he wouldn't even consider it," says one Prozac user. After several months on the drug, she went to show him the results. "You're not going to make me pay for this session," she told him.

People on Prozac feel they do, in fact, change, and a lot more tangibly than through therapy alone. One user says that all the therapy in the world hasn't made her as self-assured as Prozac has. "If somebody acts a little cold to me when I go in to work, instead of agonizing over it for hours, I think, 'Well, maybe they're having a bad day,'" she says. Another describes his reaction to bad news—hypothetically, a flat tire—to illustrate his progress. "In the past, my reaction would've been 'Ah, here we go again. Who needs it? Why me?'" he says. "Now it's 'Hell, it's just a flat tire,' and it doesn't get interpreted in such a grandiose way." And these are not mere happy vegetables. "My supervisor jumps up and down and hugs me, she's so pleased with me," says one user pursuing the Ph.D. she put off for years.

But patients' biggest defense of Prozac is that they still get depressed, a comfort to those who fear some *Brave New World* kind of high. "I had a lousy day at the office today," one woman on Prozac said. "But it didn't screw up my evening. I didn't take it with me all day." Another, talking about a deep, tired feeling of despondency, says, "That used to be my whole life; now I just have days."

Like a lot of former drug abusers, Ellis, a 50-year-old film-maker's associate, was exceedingly wary about taking any type of mood drug. Drugs and alcohol had helped him throw away a good part of his life. But since going on Prozac, he has changed his mind. "You should try everything to make your life better," he says, "and if it's legal and it works, why not?"

A Grateful Prozac User Talks to Its Creators

Tracy Thompson

The following selection, first published in 1993, is both a personal account of one person's battle with depression and an investigation and profile of the scientists who created the antidepressant Prozac. The author, *Washington Post* staff writer Tracy Thompson, vividly describes her fight with depression and her state of mind before and after taking Prozac. She then tells of her trip to the corporate headquarters of Eli Lilly and Company to visit and thank the three scientists credited with developing Prozac and to learn the process by which they first developed and tested the drug.

In my palm is a green and off-white capsule containing a white powder. Once it is swallowed, some 39 quintillion molecules of something called fluoxetine hydrochloride will migrate to my brain, where they will attach to nerve cells and prevent them from picking up serotonin, a neurotransmitter that shuttles electrical impulses from one nerve cell to another.

With less serotonin being picked up, more of it will be around up there, delivering tiny jolts of electricity from nerve to nerve. You could say this little capsule is about to ratchet up the voltage in my head. And in some way—no one knows precisely how—this will help me feel better. Happier. Without

Tracy Thompson, "The Wizard of Prozac," *The Washington Post*, November 21, 1993, pp. 73–77. Copyright © 1993 by Washington Post Book World Service/Washington Post Writers Group. Reproduced by permission.

anxiety. Able to take pleasure in ordinary things. Sane. And therein lies one of the more intriguing medical controversies of our time.

A New Drug

The drug is called Prozac, and since it came on the U.S. market in 1988 it has proved to be a startlingly effective treatment for the common but potentially deadly mental illness known as depression. More than 12 million people around the world have taken it so far. For Eli Lilly and Co., sales of Prozac brought in more than $1.1 billion in 1993, testimony to the drug's broad medical acceptance.

Prozac is different from anything that has come before. It is not a sedative or a euphoriant, and it does not have the side effects associated with the first antidepressants developed in the late 1950s.

Yet something about it seems scary. Since 1990, Lilly has been dogged by lawsuits claiming that, for some vulnerable patients, Prozac triggered homicidal or suicidal impulses. The evidence has yet [as of 1993] to convince any court of law, and the medical debate has largely yielded to a disquieting philosophical one.

Prozac fundamentally and selectively alters personality without altering perception. This gives rise to disturbing questions: By using Prozac, are we fiddling with the human soul? Does the drug's effectiveness mean that we don't *have* a soul— that the mind is merely a glob of tissue in which electrical and chemical events occur?

It comes down to this: Who am I? Am I my no-chemicals-added self, no matter how unhappy I may be? Or should I swallow this pill, achieve tranquillity and risk obliterating a certain essential part of me?

Some consider this a paralyzing moral dilemma. I don't. For me, having lived through episodes of major depression, this is a no-brainer. If there is a pill that will make you well, or make it less likely you will get sick, you take it. If Prozac hasn't saved my life, it has profoundly changed it. But there are times when I have the uneasy sense that I am ceding a big part of my autonomy to the pharmaceutical industry. I wonder who I would be if I weren't taking Prozac. Maybe I would be a tortured genius, like [the romantic poet] Lord Byron. Or maybe I would be just me, with periods of dank despondency.

Describing Depression

Describing depression is difficult. It's a complex illness with symptoms ranging from anxiety attacks, inability to concentrate, irritability, weight loss or gain and sleep disturbances to its best-known sign: a deep, chronic sense of emptiness and despair.

Like all mental illness, depression exiles people into a foreign territory of the mind. I kept a travel diary from age 14, a journal that filled up dozens of spiral-bound notebooks. It was my way of trying to make sense of The Beast, as I came to call it, which sat on my chest at night and rode my back during the day.

"Inside, I am a battlefield—Waterloo after Napoleon, Vicksburg after the siege," I wrote in the spring of my 20th year. "Always a war; always fighting one emotion or another."

On a summer night that year, a mockingbird kept me awake singing outside my window. I was sure he was mocking me—flaunting his music in the sticky-warm air, reminding me that it was 4 A.M. and that I had not slept for hours, that soon I would have to get up and face another day of deadening duties and crushing sadness. Exhausted but wide awake, I lay in the sweat-damp bedsheets, unable for the life of me to remember why I was sad.

Throughout the year that followed, I felt myself leaving the people I loved. They stood on the shore, growing smaller and indistinct, as I drifted away on my reluctant journey. I felt trapped in an invisible, airless chamber, my frantic gestures ignored or misunderstood. To others, I merely seemed remote and angry.

After many months, the episode ended as imperceptibly as it had begun. But there would be others. I found a psychiatrist, and eventually tried antidepressants, but in doses too small to do me any good. Not surprisingly, the relief I got was fleeting.

Trying Prozac

It was not until 1990 that I tried Prozac. I had been vacationing with friends on Cape Cod. It was August, six months after I had been hospitalized for the most severe episode of depression yet. I still wasn't well.

After a week at the beach, a sudden panic at the approach of my 35th birthday made me bolt; to the bafflement of my friends, I left and checked into a motel. There, I spent one of the worst nights of my life, wondering if The Beast had won after all, if the moment had come to negotiate a surrender.

In the morning, at the urging of my psychiatrist, I caught a plane to Washington, D.C. A prescription for Prozac was waiting for me at my neighborhood drugstore.

Two days later, while at home, I had a moment of what I can only call clearheadedness. The suffocating anxiety was gone, momentarily, and I felt a deep relief, a sense of sudden calm after eons of warfare inside my head. I had gotten so used to the noise that the quiet was unfamiliar. It was as if the evil beast that had been holding my head under water, trying to drown me, had suddenly let go.

There were still several weeks in which I found it hard to concentrate or sleep, and in which the daily weight of sadness seemed too much to drag around with me. But by October I definitely knew: I was better. I have been taking Prozac ever since. I am, you might say, chemically altered.

Exactly what form this alteration has taken, I will never know. I don't feel sedated, jittery or drugged. I simply feel normal—as if I had been driving a car all these years with the parking brake on, and now it is off. I feel as if the real me has returned, perhaps all the way from childhood, where she lived before The Beast arrived.

Sometimes I sense that I have lost an intensity of feeling along with the moments of lacerating despair. I have greedily swapped them for ordinary life. That may sound dull, but I tell you it is sweet. It is not caviar I crave, but clean sheets and hot soup.

At some point, the thought came to me that few people have affected my life quite as profoundly as the person who invented this drug. And I decided to tell him so, whoever and wherever he was. Which is how I came to search for the Wizard of Prozac.

Visiting the Prozac Scientists

Eli Lilly's corporate headquarters—a 90-acre complex of offices and laboratories—rises Ozlike out of the flat Indiana farmland. The Lilly public-relations department scheduled an exhaustive tour, the highlight of which would be my meeting with the Prozac scientists.

It turned out that the wizard I sought was not one person, but three: Ray Fuller, David Wong and Bryan Molloy. Besides these three who collect the awards, I was informed, hundreds of people at Lilly worked on the Prozac project for more than 15 years. The era of solitary Pasteurs puttering up miracles in their labs is as obsolete as the Model T.

Fuller and Wong are unassuming, middle-aged men who convey a genial, pastoral demeanor—a bit like small-town family doctors. Molloy is different: quirky, irascible, he keeps to himself in offices on the other side of the Lilly complex. He has a gaunt, angular face and a discernible trace of Scotland in his speech. He seems intense, at home between his own two ears, impatient with social niceties.

Molloy gave me an abbreviated version of how Prozac was developed. The idea was simple: instead of examining existing drugs to discover which ones had antidepressant side effects, Molloy decided to start with the side effect and build a drug that would trigger it. It was the scientific method in reverse— as if Molloy had decided to write a mystery novel with the ending in the first chapter.

Molloy started in 1971 with a trip to Lilly's chemical library, the vast collection of compounds the company keeps in its vaults for research purposes. Antihistamines had yielded the first major antidepressant drugs, so Molloy started with compounds whose chemical structures resembled antihistamines.

He knew which neurotransmitters he wanted to leave alone—those that produced grogginess and dry mouth, among other side effects—but he was not sure which ones he wanted to target. Several years before, he and Fuller had collaborated on research involving serotonin, and Fuller was by this point convinced that serotonin was an important neurotransmitter in the brain and was linked to depression.

It was Wong, working independently, who supplied the last, crucial link in the developmental chain. Using ground-up brain cells of rats, he created a precise test for measuring the uptake of serotonin in brain cells.

Less than two years after Molloy started, Wong's tests confirmed that one compound Molloy and Fuller had created, known as LY110140, had a potent and selective effect only on serotonin. This was Prozac.

Fuller quoted one of his scientific predecessors, neurophysiologist Ralph Gerard: "Behind every crooked thought there lies a crooked molecule." So, I asked, is there a chemical for every sadness?

Sadness and Chemistry

No, he said, but every sadness is chemical. There was an experiment in which damselfish were kept in a tank with only a transparent wall between them and some predator fish. The damselfish had every reason to think they were about to be eaten. After a while, the serotonin levels in their brains showed a marked change. It's illustrative, in a crude way, Fuller said. Loss, anxiety, repeated rejection—"things we experience do cause neurochemical changes in the brain."

The most important question, the one I had gone to Indiana to ask, I put to Molloy. After all, it was Molloy who started everything, more than 20 years ago.

How does it make you feel, I asked, to know that you have helped people? To know that this molecule you discovered has allowed me to live my life in a way I never thought possible?

There was an awkward pause. "I'm happy for you, okay?" He clearly wished I were not there, asking that sentimental, unscientific question. What came out, finally, was so stunningly honest that I did not know what to say, and so I said nothing.

"I just wanted to do it for the intellectual high," he said. "It looked like scientific fun."

Reality is rarely what we imagine. Great and noble things do not always happen for great and noble reasons.

I can live with that. Happily ever after.

The Prozac Backlash

Denise Grady

By the time the following selection was first published in 1990, Prozac had become one of the most popular prescribed drugs of all time. In less than three years since its introduction, more than 2 million people had used the antidepressant. However, headlines about Prozac's side effects were beginning to replace previous stories about the miraculous wonder drug. Writer Denise Grady describes the controversy about Prozac that emerged in the early 1990s. Some patients were complaining that the drug had made them feel worse or even suicidal; others blamed the drug for incidents of violent behavior. Grady also discusses several lawsuits that were filed against Eli Lilly and Company, the corporation selling Prozac. A freelance writer when this article was published, Denise Grady later became a health and medicine reporter for the *New York Times.*

On July 17 [1990], a 40-year-old woman named Rhonda Hala filed a $150 million lawsuit against Eli Lilly and Company, charging that Lilly's phenomenally successful antidepressant drug, Prozac, had made her slash herself more than 150 times and try repeatedly to commit suicide. A psychiatrist had prescribed Prozac for Hala in October 1988, when she became depressed after back surgery and withdrawal from painkillers. She was also taking Xanax, a tranquilizer. Hala says she had never thought of killing herself before, but after a few weeks on Prozac she turned violently suicidal, and remained that way, off and on, for a year and a half—until the psychiatrist learned that Prozac might be the cause, and took her off it. Hala, who

Denise Grady, "Wonder Drug/Killer Drug," *American Health*, vol. 9, October 1990, pp. 60–65. Copyright © 1990 by Denise Grady. Reproduced by permission.

lives in Shirley, NY, with her husband and two children, says she hasn't had a self-destructive thought since.

Hala's lawyer, Leonard Finz, called a press conference to announce the lawsuit. Prozac, Finz said, had not been tested properly before it was marketed. The media picked up on the controversy at once, one TV station featuring shots of Hala pointing out her scars.

The next day, Jerrold S. Parker, an attorney with Finz's firm, said the office telephones were "ringing off the hook." Hundreds of other people who had taken Prozac wanted to sue. "Some of them cut toes off or carved words in their chests," said Parker. "Some sat on railroad tracks, hanged or shot themselves, or emptied out their medicine chests and poured the contents down their throats. If you can think of a way to commit suicide, that's what they've been doing. Every call is another adventure."

Many of the potential clients, Parker added, seemed to be "pretty solid people—maybe depressed, but they had never dreamed of suicide." He and Finz monitored Hala's press interviews; by the end of the week, Parker had also heard from the families of "hundreds" of patients who had attemped suicide or actually killed themselves while taking Prozac. Meanwhile, a week after Hala filed suit, three families of victims murdered by a Louisville, KY, man who shot 20 people and then killed himself while taking Prozac and other drugs also sued Lilly for $50 million each. They're claiming it was Prozac that caused the man's violent behavior.

From Wonder Drug to Suicide Pill

Prozac? Just last winter [in 1989], the cover stories were ecstatic: *New York* magazine billed it as the wonder drug for depression, *Newsweek* called it a breakthrough. Patient after patient felt good after years of despair—not high or drugged, just normal. Marriages were saved, careers rescued: Prozac, also called fluoxetine, was giving people back their lives. Typically, there was no price to pay, because Prozac, unlike other antidepressants, had minimal side effects. The case histories were so exciting that even readers who had never been depressed couldn't help wondering if Prozac might help them feel better. "I had people come in clutching *Newsweek* and saying, 'I want to be on this medication,'" says one psychiatrist.

In less than three years on the market, Prozac beat out more than a dozen older drugs to become the nation's most-prescribed antidepressant and one of the best-selling drugs of all time. The market for such drugs is vast: The National Institute of Mental Health estimates that 10.5 million Americans suffer from depressive illness—not just sadness, but a real disease, a chemical imbalance in the brain. Some 2 million people worldwide have already taken Prozac, and pharmacists have been filling more than 500,000 prescriptions a month—even though it costs $1.50 a pill, several times the cost of many other antidepressants. Industry analysts have estimated that Prozac sales totaled $350 million in 1989 and will double yearly; they were expected to reach $700 million this year [1990] and $1 billion by 1991.

The FDA has approved it only for depression, but it's being tested for other psychiatric conditions, and also as a weight-loss aid, though Lilly won't discuss the research. Even though the studies aren't completed, doctors have already prescribed Prozac for dieters and psychiatric problems other than depression, including obsessive-compulsive disorder, bulimia and panic attacks.

Now, as the headlines switch from "wonder drug" to "suicide pill," Prozac's future seems unclear. FDA officials and leading psychiatrists insist that the horror stories are rare, and that Prozac has helped far more people than it may have harmed. Dr. Jack Gorman, director of biological studies at Columbia University's College of Physicians and Surgeons, worries that overblown publicity about suicide will "scare people away from a good drug." But the idea of suicide as a side effect of a medication, however rare, may be unacceptable to the public. Support groups for "Prozac survivors" have sprung up in six states, and more are being formed. Some members claim the drug made them want to kill other people as well as themselves. Finz's law firm, which specializes in drug liability, is signing up new clients practically every day, and Finz says he hopes to see Prozac taken off the market.

For now, the number of lawsuits doesn't mean much: They may or may not hold up. "One lawsuit gets reported and you start having suits all over the place," says Gorman. "People are going to try to make a fortune out of this."

Given that 30,000 Americans a year were killing themselves before Prozac came along, it may be hard to prove that patients became suicidal from Prozac and not from depression itself. Indeed, Lilly has a prepared statement quoting from a medical text that claims the rate of suicide for depressed patients is 22 to 36 times that of the general public. The company refuses to discuss any lawsuits, but spokesmen acknowledge that doctors were informed by letter in May [1990] that suicidal thoughts and violent behavior had been "temporally" though not "causally" associated with Prozac in some patients.

Side Effects Emerge

Some experts wonder whether Prozac survivors are the victims of bad doctoring rather than a bad drug: People taking any psychiatric medication are supposed to be monitored closely, and those who get worse are supposed to be taken off the drug fast. Hala, for instance, stayed on Prozac for a year and a half, yet she's suing Lilly, not her doctor.

What is happening to Prozac could have happened to nearly any new drug that so quickly became popular and widely regarded as extraordinarily safe. With all new drugs, side effects not detected during testing almost always emerge in the first few years of use, simply because more people take the drug.

"You always learn more about a drug once it's on the mar-

ket, beyond what was learned in clinical trials," says Dr. Norman Sussman, director of psychiatric residency training at
New York University Medical Center, who has treated 150 patients with Prozac. But Prozac's wonder-drug reputation set
up such grandiose expectations that when the inevitable problems arose it was as if the national trust had been betrayed.

During the past year, Prozac has made its way onto the hit
list of the Citizens Commission on Human Rights (CCHR)—a
group founded by the Church of Scientology to campaign
against the "psychiatric industry," and the use of psychiatric
drugs. CCHR solicits affidavits from people who have had bad
experiences with medication, and maintains that the drugs
make people psychotic and violent. The group investigates
murder cases, and when it finds psychiatric drugs involved,
generally blames the drug for the crime. During [1990], CCHR
has identified several murderers who were taking Prozac, and
has helped connect newspaper and TV reporters—including
Geraldo Rivera—with people who have had bad reactions to
the drug. CCHR's role isn't always mentioned, so audiences
have no idea who's helping to generate the bad press. Material supplied by the group was among the information Hala's
lawyers handed out to reporters.

What made Prozac so popular in the first place was not its
effectiveness. Despite all the media hype, Prozac, like other
antidepressants, helps only 60% to 70% of the depressed patients who try it, notes Dr. Jerrold Rosenbaum, chief of the
clinical psychopharmacology unit at Massachusetts General
Hospital in Boston. The charm was that, initially at least, it did
appear to have hardly any side effects for most patients—a far
cry from older antidepressants. "The older drugs had side effects that were so distressing or dangerous in some cases that
it was very difficult to get patients to comply with a full course
of therapy," adds Sussman.

The "older drugs" are two other classes of antidepressants:
The tricyclics include drugs such as Elavil and Tofranil, and the
monoamine oxidase inhibitors, or MAOI's, include Nardil and

THE HISTORY OF DRUGS

How Prozac Almost Killed Me

The 1995 book Living with Prozac and Other Selective Serotonin Reuptake Inhibitors *featured personal stories of people who had taken antidepressants for their depression. In this excerpt, Lindsay Windsor tells of her negative experiences with Prozac.*

My severe depression began in 1991 when my mother became seriously ill with throat cancer. Watching her attempt to overcome it with chemotherapy, surgeries, and radiation implants, until there was nothing more to be done for her except the insertion of a stomach tube so that she could simply survive, nearly destroyed me. The inexplicable pain I felt after she died was more than I could bear because I had to be so strong for her during her illness.

I sought the help of a psychiatrist earlier this year when I could no longer live with the pain and hopelessness and had become a complete recluse. He prescribed Elavil on the basis that it had helped me once before. It didn't this time. . . . Then came my near-fatal experience with Prozac.

My doctor prescribed the usual dose of 20 mg., and I took it just as it was prescribed. In only one week on Prozac, I steadily went downhill to find myself in the most severe, suicidal depression I have ever known. During a follow-up visit with a surgeon (I had had nasal surgery in May), I completely broke down, sobbing hysterically, totally out of control. Upon returning home, I threw some eighty Prozac pills down the toilet. It was either that or I was going to end my life.

I immediately went to see my psychiatrist and told him that taking Prozac was without a doubt my worst nightmare ever. I felt that I was losing my mind. I have never known such confusion, inescapable pain, and suffering. I felt out of touch with reality. After three to four days, I gradually returned to my old self, still depressed but certainly not as severely. Prozac was not for me, ever!

Lindsay Windsor, in *Living with Prozac and Other Selective Serotonin Reuptake Inhibitors: Personal Accounts of Life on Antidepressants*. Ed. Debra Elfenbein. San Francisco: HarperSanFrancisco, 1995.

Parnate. Both classes can cause weight gain and sedation; the tricyclics can also produce dry mouth, constipation and heart rhythm disturbances. Also, for people on MAOI's certain foods are taboo.

"In addition," says Sussman, "with tricyclics in particular, you have to increase the doses gradually, because of the side effects, and build up over several weeks to get into the therapeutic range. But many patients can't tolerate full doses, and take levels that are too low. So probably fewer are getting better."

With Prozac, Sussman says, "Many patients have no side effects at all. Generally, people can tolerate this drug. And everybody starts with the full-strength, 20-milligram capsule." That can be increased to as much as 80 mg a day if the usual low dose doesn't seem to help. The drug can take a month or so to work (and as long to clear from the body) but many patients respond sooner. Doctors have been more comfortable prescribing Prozac than other drugs, adds Sussman.

"Most people don't go to psychiatrists," he says. "It's mostly family practitioners and internists who treat depression, and most have been timid about prescribing antidepressants. They tend to underdose. Prozac has had such impact because people are taking enough to get better. I could tell you stories about people who are ready to jump out a window, and then after eight days on Prozac they say they've never felt better. It's probably made more of an impact on people's lives than just about any other drug. It's terrific."

For a small but significant minority of patients, though, Prozac has always been known to cause certain side effects. It provokes distressing reactions, mainly anxiety and agitation, in as many as 15% of patients. In addition, Sussman says, "Some develop headaches or nausea; others have real stubborn insomnia; and some lose their sexual desire or the ability to have an orgasm. The frequency of sexual dysfunction surprises me—it seems higher than reported in the premarketing studies."

As for the reports of suicidal impulses, Sussman notes that

the numbers have been small. One of his patients did feel suicidal more than a year ago. Sussman immediately assumed Prozac might be the cause—something any good psychiatrist should do, he says—and took the patient off the drug. "But other antidepressants can do that as well," he says. "It doesn't happen often enough to deter you from using the drug, but patients do have to monitored and seen frequently."

Can Prozac Make People Suicidal?

The possibility that Prozac might make some people suicidal was first raised in a paper published last February [1990] in the *American Journal of Psychiatry* by Dr. Martin Teicher, an associate professor of psychiatry at Harvard. Teicher's report concerned only six patients, but his findings were disturbing. They convinced Hala's psychiatrist to take her off Prozac, and the paper has since become key evidence in her case against Lilly. Teicher has also been asked to act as a consultant by lawyers for the family of one of the people murdered by the Louisville man on Prozac.

Teicher's six patients, he wrote, "developed intense, violent, suicidal preoccupation after two to seven weeks of fluoxetine treatment." Although several had contemplated suicide before starting Prozac, none of them had ever experienced such a powerful urge toward self-destruction as they did while taking the drug. Some became obsessed with specific, violent methods: turning on gas jets to blow up an apartment, driving into a bridge abutment, blowing their brains out. Those feelings lasted three days to three months after they got off Prozac. Soon after the paper came out, Teicher received reports of a dozen such cases, including three patients who actually did kill themselves. He worries that nonpsychiatrists who prescribe Prozac may not realize emotional changes could be due to the drug.

Teicher thinks the severe effects, though they may be exceedingly rare, are real. "As a scientist, it's easy to remain skeptical and say it hasn't been proved, one should rechallenge these patients with Prozac and see if it happens again. But that would be largely unethical. Those who develop the extreme reaction seem very strange when they're on this medication—their thoughts are so intrusive, and completely out of character. Some of these patients I've known five or six years," says Teicher, "and I've never known them to be this way before. Take them off the drug and they say, 'How could I have thought that way? Boy, I was really feeling strange on that medication.' As a clinician, I do feel it's some strange adverse response to the medication, and not just a coincidence."

Still, Teicher prescribes Prozac for some patients, mainly those who didn't do well with the earlier drugs. "A lot of people have been on a plethora of drugs, and Prozac is the first time they have done well," he says. "If there's any motion to take this drug off the market, a lot of people will hate me for the rest of my life." Teicher warns his own patients about the possibility of emotional side effects and monitors them closely. All six in his report became intensely fatigued or lethargic on Prozac, or slept excessively; four felt intense inner restlessness. None got relief from depression. He thus suspects that people who react that way may be especially at risk for suicidal impulses. "We need a way of addressing the possible hazards," he says. Doctors and patients both need to be warned; Teicher thinks it may even be necessary to develop a formal monitoring system. "If we can build in safeguards, Prozac is a very valuable drug."

However, few other psychiatrists have had negative experiences like Teicher's. "He is an outstanding psychiatrist, but these are sporadic cases," says Columbia's Gorman. He says he hasn't seen a negative response in the many patients he has on Prozac—100 or so.

"To me," says Gorman, "the most important thing about Teicher's report is that even though Prozac is a good drug, you can't just give it to patients and tell them to come back in six months. These people are very depressed, and it may take the medication four to six weeks to work. Suicide may be the natural course of the disease."

Dr. Jerrold Rosenbaum of Massachusetts General Hospital doubts that Teicher's findings have much bearing on most patients. For one thing, Rosenbaum says, Teicher's patients were "atypical. They had long histories of treatment-resistant depression, some with complicating medical or neuropsychiatric conditions." In addition, four of the six took other drugs along with Prozac and three had recently discontinued MAOI treatment.

Rosenbaum also has data that challenge Teicher's findings. In a study of more than 1,000 patients, Rosenbaum found that people taking Prozac, or Prozac plus one of the older drugs, were slightly more likely to have suicidal thoughts than those taking just the older drugs. However, the differences weren't statistically significant, and no one experienced the obsessional preoccupation with suicide Teicher described. Moreover, Rosenbaum says, a paper published several years ago reported on four suicidal patients nearly identical to Teicher's—except that they were taking a different drug, and at least two subsequently got better on Prozac.

Some psychiatrists also believe in something they call the "rollback phenomenon," in which severely depressed patients who are recovering may retrace their steps through earlier stages of their illness—including a suicidal phase. Another way of describing this is to say that really depressed people are too incapacitated even to kill themselves, and as they start to feel better they become more capable of acting on their thoughts.

"I had one patient who had been depressed all her life," says Rosenbaum. "On Prozac, she recovered to a point she thought impossible. But she mentioned that on the third day of treatment she had several hours of suicidal thoughts. Was that the drug or the rollback phenomenon? I've had other patients who became suicidal after starting treatment and then got better on the same treatment."

FDA officials weren't alarmed by Teicher's report because the number of patients studied was so small compared with the enormous number of Prozac users, and because some were taking other drugs too, says Dr. Paul Leber, head of the FDA division that monitors psychiatric drugs. Moreover, the many suicides reported by Hala's lawyers don't match up with what has been reported to the FDA. "Teicher's patients told him they felt suicidal, but they didn't kill themselves," adds Leber. "That can be a healthy sign." Finally, he notes, Teicher's report may have suffered from "ascertainment bias": If you discover a specific symptom, and look for it again, you tend to find it.

Similarly, Leber says, the more than 8,900 negative reports received on Prozac haven't caused much worry at the agency, even though that number is unusually high. Given the extensive use of Prozac, its newness and all the publicity, he says, "The numbers are not surprising to us at all. Reporting tends to decrease over the years as people get used to the drug." The FDA is continuously monitoring Prozac and the adverse reports, but has found no "unreasonable or unexpected risk" associated with it.

Ignorance of How Prozac Works

If one glaring bit of ignorance lies at the heart of the controversy, it is that nobody knows exactly how Prozac, or any antidepressant, works in the brain. It is believed that depressed people have abnormal brain levels of certain neurotransmitters, chemicals that are released from one nerve cell to signal another. In some cases of depression, the neurotransmitter serotonin seems to be especially scarce. Extremely low levels have been found in some people who committed suicide. Unlike other antidepressants, which act on several neurotransmitters at once, Prozac specifically prolongs serotonin's effects by preventing the nerve cells from reabsorbing it.

But serotonin affects many different sites in the brain, and not all its actions are understood. Some people may be hypersensitive to the increased serotonin activity Prozac induces, which might lead to agitation and anxiety. In addition, Prozac can gradually change brain-cell sensitivity to the neurotransmitter, so people's reactions to the drug may change with time. Prozac's powerful, highly selective action on serotonin troubles Teicher. "What we've learned recently is that over the course of time, other drugs affecting serotonin can have irreversible consequences," he says. "The drug Ecstasy [MDMA] seems to permanently damage serotonin nerve terminals. Fenfluramine, which has been given to autistic kids and used as an appetite suppressant, may have a similar effect. Animal studies show both drugs to be fairly potent neurotoxins. "There is no hint that Prozac is neurotoxic in people or animals," Teicher says. Still, the biochemistry worries him.

What especially concerns Teicher is that there's a lot of interest in using Prozac for children and adolescents. "Believe me, they suffer from severe depression, and suicide is a major problem in adolescents," he says. "They can't tolerate the other antidepressants very well, and teenagers are also prone to overdosing." Because Prozac is relatively safe in an overdose, he says, "It looks very useful." But the drug has never been tested in children, "so all the information is anecdotal."

Teicher's concern about the possibility of neurotoxicity is "reasonable," says Gorman, "but I think the chances of a permanent effect after a few years are very small. The dilemma is, people can get depressed again when you take them off Prozac, but we don't know what might happen if you keep them on it forever."

So far, Prozac seems to be a useful, if imperfect drug whose strengths and weaknesses have *both* been blown out of proportion. It must be measured against the condition it was developed to treat. "Depression is horrible," says Gorman. "People die from it, including children."

"There are real risks to treatment," Rosenbaum adds, "but the risks of nontreatment are much greater. I'm sure with any antidepressant you can find hundreds of cases where the effects were disastrous—overdoses, allergies, side effects—but there are many more cases where treatment prevents people from committing suicide and allows them to lead a normal life." For those with genuine depression, Rosenbaum says, the benefits of Prozac usually outweigh the risks. "But people shouldn't be taking it just because they're feeling a little blue."

The final chapters in the story of this putative wonder drug remain to be written. But it looks as though Prozac's future may be decided by litigation and headlines, instead of research and physicians.

A Widespread Culture of Prozac Users

Nathan Cobb

During the 1990s the antidepressant Prozac became so popular in the United States that it provoked discussion on how it was affecting American culture. In the following article, first published in 1994, Nathan Cobb examines what he calls a "culture of Prozacians." He writes that Prozac was becoming as ubiquitous in American society as Valium had been in the 1960s. Millions of people, not all of whom were clinically depressed, were taking Prozac to improve their mental well-being and were openly talking about it with friends and associates. Cobb's article includes a discussion with Peter D. Kramer, a psychiatrist whose 1993 book, *Listening to Prozac*, attained best-seller status and established Kramer as a spokesperson for the drug. Cobb is a correspondent for the *Boston Globe*.

All is not tranquil within the pastel land of Prozac. Missives of discontent are being sent forth from the pale pink headquarters of Eli Lilly and Co., the Indianapolis-based developer of the best-selling antidepressant. The word according to Lilly, being disseminated in part through an unusual new advertising campaign, is that much of the media attention surrounding the drug has "trivialized" clinical depression by suggesting that people also take Prozac for lesser conditions.

But wait. Listening to users talk about Prozac, you soon learn that the common thread is that there isn't a common thread, other than the drug itself. A kind of widespread culture of Prozacians seems to have developed. Many of its populace are indeed depressed, some hover on the edge of depression and a few are simply trying to jump-start their moods. You hear lots of different stories on the Prozac trail. There's the clinical psychiatric specialist in Somerville, Mass., who announces that Prozac has splintered the weight of depression from her shoulders like a wrecking ball. There's the health care worker in Jamaica Plain who claims he uses Prozac as a kind of pep pill to combat fatigue. There's the editor in Cambridge who cuts the drug with Xanax, an antianxiety medication, because she doesn't think Prozac does the whole job. And then there's the writer who stopped taking it because it made her incapable of achieving orgasm.

"Some things," muses this last woman, "are worse than being depressed."

Still, the notion of rather broad-based use of Prozac troubles Lilly. "We don't want people to confuse someone with a serious medical problem with someone who has one or two 'down' days," explains Dr. Gary Tollefson, executive director of the CNS (for central nervous system) unit within the company. "We don't want everyone lumped together." Yet a company spokesman who contends that the vast majority of people taking the drug are doing so for clinical depression—one of two conditions it has been approved to treat—also says that the firm can't release available statistical data on the reasons people use Prozac.

What Lilly will say is that about 10 million folks have taken the drug (roughly two-thirds of them women), thereby making it the most popular antidepressant ever. Much as they did with Valium during the 1960s, people openly mention the P word in restaurants, car pools, saloons, checkout lines and waiting rooms. Prozac—as seen on T-shirts, talk shows and magazine covers—has become a household brand name that enjoys the familiarity of Pepsi. Judith Winters of Cambridge takes Prozac, and so do three of her friends. "We talk about it to each other," she says. "A lot." Winters describes herself as seriously depressed since adolescence, a woman who has lost a number of administrative jobs because of her inability to hold herself together. Prozac, she explains, has allowed her to function, and without the side effect—severe thirst—she experienced with imipramine, an antidepressant she took previously. She no longer bursts into tears in public, no longer spends weeks on end inside her apartment. "When you're depressed," she says, "fun is simply not a concept you can understand."

Al Peters says that he has been taking Prozac on and off for about a year and a half. Although he doesn't think the drug is necessarily a substitute for talk therapy, he, too, is a satisfied customer. Yet his case is considerably different from Winters'. "I was a guy who was simply always down," says the retired dentist and avid skier who lives in Glen, N.H. "Gloomy. Saw the glass as half empty, not half full. My work wasn't being affected, but the quality of my life and my interpersonal relationships were. Prozac doesn't make me euphoric, but it gives me a feeling of well-being. It makes me happy within my skin."

Good or Bad?

Is Prozac a good thing? Ah, there we go: We want it to be either white magic or black magic, wonder drug or witches' brew. In truth, the relatively fast-acting green and white capsules seem to be many things to many people. "The range of things you can use it for is absolutely incredible," says Dr. John Pearce, a local psychiatrist and Prozac enthusiast who says he has treated hundreds of patients with the drug. Pearce's list includes panic disorders, anxiety disorders, obsessive-compulsive disorders (the second condition for which the drug has been approved by the FDA), post-traumatic stress disorders, and eating disorders.

"Everything," Pearce effuses, "but psychosis."

Prozac is nothing if not tenacious. Popular wisdom has it that the drug suffered from a temporary backlash in 1990 after reports that it induced violent and suicidal tendencies in some users, but you couldn't tell it by sales figures compiled by Lilly.

The laboratory-designed drug, which was a decade and a half in the making by Lilly scientists, hasn't had a down year, saleswise, since it was released at the end of 1987. Last year [1993] it was a $1.2 billion business, $880 million of that in the United States. Sales of the world's most popular antidepressant are expected to increase a healthy 12 percent this year [1994].

It doesn't seem to matter that Prozac has never been tested for its addictive potential or that its long-term risks are unknown. Its side effects—including headache, nervousness, insomnia, anxiety and reduced sex drive—are generally benign when compared to those of earlier generations of antidepressants. This has made even family physicians eager to prescribe it, especially for dysthymia, aka low-end depression. "It's very good for run-of-the-mill depression," contends Dr. Michael Lowney, who says he's had about an 80 percent success rate with Prozac in his Boston family practice. "That means people who can't cope, who are used to being successful but whose depression is significant enough to interfere with their lifestyle."

Dr. Asha Wallace, a family practitioner in Needham, prescribes Prozac to women with both PMS and what she describes as "a bluesy feeling." Says Wallace: "They feel they're not coping, they're stressed, they have a sense of sadness, they have too much to do just holding things together. I don't call it dysthymia. I call it more of a range of normal feelings that are bordering on depression."

One Person's Story

Consider Erica Faldt. Nursing a cup of hot apple cider in a Boston coffee house recently, Faldt is explaining that Prozac was prescribed for her by her psychiatrist about four months ago. "I'm not sure if he ever used the word 'depression,'" says the 25-year-old student as she leans across the small table. Her eyes widen. "I'm not sick."

Instead, Faldt explains, she was lacking both will and focus. She was also feeling, as she puts it, "gray and moody." Besides, she had recently moved to the United States from her native Sweden. "Here, it's a very fast-paced life," she says. "People are supposed to produce. Sweden is a much smaller and slower country. You're not expected to be so productive. And you can take time to look at your emotional life. We have a tradition of melancholy there. Here, if you're depressed, you're weird."

For about three weeks after she began taking Prozac, Faldt recalls, she felt constantly nauseated. She was tired. She lost her appetite. And then . . . "We have a word for it in Sweden," she says. "Handlingskraftig. It means you have the power to act. I feel stronger now. I used to be shy, a little introverted. Now I'm feeling more outgoing, more social, more adventurous. And I'm much more organized. I do better in school. I've changed."

Still, Faldt isn't sure she's comfortable with the notion of chemical alteration. "In some ways I feel I've lost contact with the center of me," she explains. "I'm not as thinking, not as serious. I'm happy, but this seems like a kind of cosmetic solution. It sounds schizophrenic, but I think that was the real me back then (i.e., pre-Prozac). This is me being constantly happy. And I'm a little worried that I won't like this OK person."

Whether Faldt has traded in her old personality as she might a cranky Saab is a question that makes Prozac a hot topic for meditation and disagreement.

Not even Lilly claims to know exactly why its prize product works, only that it is the first of a new class of drugs that selectively blocks the reabsorption of a neurotransmitter known as serotonin, and that serotonin is somehow involved in regulating mood. So the debate persists: Does Prozac change behavior or personality?

The Voice of Prozac

In a bright yellow Federalist house located on College Hill on the East Side of Providence, lives someone for whom Prozac has caused a kind of sea change. Funny, though: Dr. Peter Kramer has never taken the drug. (He adds sheepishly that he can count on the fingers of one hand the number of times he's had two drinks.) "I'm a worrier," he replies when asked why he hasn't sampled Prozac. "I'm a worrier about the long-term side effects."

Even so, the boyish-looking 45-year-old psychiatrist, who also teaches at Brown University, has become the voice of Prozac. Roughly 300,000 copies of his best-selling book, *Listening to Prozac*, have been printed since it was published last June [1993]. An earlier Kramer book, about psychiatry in the technological age, sold "3,000 copies at best."

"I find myself rather frazzled by this," says the father of three as he sits in a blue wing-back chair in his tidy period living room, referring to the fact he has been interviewed some 250 times in the past nine months. "I'm a person who likes to quietly write in the morning and quietly see patients in the afternoon." Now his telephone answering machine is filled with messages from strangers, their disembodied voices telling him that he is everything from a guru to a jerk.

Although Kramer contends that both he and his book are ambivalent about Prozac, he has been cast in the role of a kind of latter-day Timothy Leary, the 1960s figure who beat the drums for LSD. Kramer apparently did coin the term "cosmetic psychopharmacology," and he does suggest that Prozac alters personality as well as illness in a substantial minority of users who take it as a sort of mental tonic.

"Actually," he says, "I don't prescribe Prozac very much. But I have had occasion to put people on it. And they've done very well in ways one could narrowly characterize as a response to depression, but could also be characterized more broadly as personality change. And that's a wonderful thing to see." Kramer says that Prozac users are a heterogeneous bunch. "The notion that it treats only depression will be shown to be not true in the near future," he contends. "Research trends will show that Prozac goes far beyond treating depression and far beyond treating people who are ill at all." He talks about "A certain type of audience: fairly healthy . . .

productive people . . . troubled, long-suffering . . . borderline depressive . . . not readily diagnosable in the regular psychiatric scheme."

Personality Transplant

Someone like Peter Paris? When Paris turned up at Massachusetts General Hospital for help in 1990, he would certainly have called himself "troubled" and "long-suffering." But depressed? "Anxious," the 53-year-old Paris stresses, his voice cracking over the telephone line from Florida, where he moved from Gofftown, N.H., six months ago. "I just used to get, oh boy, very anxious, restless and aggressive. Like, if someone blew their horn at me, I'd get out of the car and rip into them."

Before he met Prozac, Paris, a former welder, hadn't worked for a decade. A few small real estate investments had kept him financially afloat. "I couldn't handle a job," he recalls. "You did things my way, or no way. I'd get jumpy. I'd get this tightness in the stomach. I'd get very nasty."

On Prozac, Paris says, he changed. The tightly coiled knots of anxiety have disappeared. He got a job—selling cars, no less. He even got married. "To this day, people know when I don't take a pill," he says. "They say, 'Hey, you're getting jumpy. Take your pill!'"

So what's really changed? Peter Paris' behavior or his personality?

"That's a good question," he answers. "I would have to say Prozac changed my personality. I would have to say it really did."

A true believer, Peter Paris. A loyal Prozacian. Especially after his doctor took him off Prozac for a while and put him on Zoloft, another selective serotonin reuptake inhibitor.

"It's a very nice pill, Zoloft," Paris is willing to concede. "But I'll tell you this: It's not Prozac."

Prozac and Other Antidepressants Have Changed the Practice of Psychiatry

Samuel H. Barondes

Samuel H. Barondes is a professor of neurobiology and psychiatry at the University of California at San Francisco. His works include *Molecules and Mental Illness* and *Better than Prozac: Creating the Next Generation of Psychiatric Drugs*. The following selection is taken from a 1994 article in the journal *Science*, in which he describes how Prozac and other selective serotonin reuptake inhibitors (SSRIs) have changed how psychiatrists treat people with behavioral disorders. Instead of relying solely on talk therapy to treat less severe behavioral disorders, psychiatrists are more willing to prescribe drugs such as Prozac. Barondes concludes that more research is needed to find out how Prozac and other antidepressants affect the brain.

Modern psychopharmacology was born in the 1950s with the introduction of two drugs still in wide use today. First chlorpromazine, originally an antihistamine, was unexpectedly found to alleviate symptoms of schizophrenia. Then imipramine, initially considered an alternative to chlorpromazine, was observed to alter the course of major depression. Both drugs interact with proteins that bind to specifc amine neuro-

Samuel H. Barondes, "Thinking About Prozac," *Science*, vol. 263, February 25, 1994, pp. 1,102–1,104. Copyright © 1994 by the American Association for the Advancement of Science. Reproduced by permission of the publisher and the author.

transmitters in the brain, thereby providing molecular targets for new drugs with superior properties and different applications. Among these is a descendant of imipramine, fluoxetine (marketed as Prozac by Eli Lilly), which is now widely prescribed not only for depression but also to help people cope with a range of less serious but highly prevalent behavioral symptoms. The value of Prozac and other drugs for problems that had previously been viewed as best suited for psychological treatments has, in turn, stimulated a rethinking of a fundamental assumption in psychiatry.

These developments are traceable to the early discovery that imipramine acts on membrane transporters that remove the neurotransmitters norepinephrine or serotonin from the synaptic cleft, thereby terminating their action. We now know that each of the neurotransmitters interacts with a specific transporter and that imipramine blocks both. This finding provided pharmaceutical companies with a strategy for the development of alternative drugs in order to compete in the huge market that imipramine opened. Eventually, compounds were found that selectively blocked the serotonin (but not the norepinephrine) transporter and yet were equally effective in alleviating major depression. The advantage of these new drugs [called selective serotonin reuptake inhibitors (SSRIs)] is that they lack some of the undesirable side effects of imipramine, such as dry mouth and abnormal heart rhythms. Members of this class of drugs, now available for prescription, include sertraline, paroxetine, fluvoxamine, and the current big winner—Prozac.

Prozac was introduced for clinical use in 1986 and has already been prescribed for more than 10 million people. Its popularity as an antidepressant derives not from its efficacy, which is no greater than that of imipramine, but instead from its less objectionable side effects. Not only are patients more willing to take Prozac, but it is also much less toxic than imipramine in large doses and therefore poses less danger as a potential instrument for suicide.

But the impact of Prozac has been even greater than these

advantages imply. Like imipramine, which is also helpful in preventing the severe anxiety attacks of patients with panic disorder and the repetitive intrusive thoughts and uncontrollable rituals of patients with obsessive-compulsive disorder, Prozac has been used in the treatment of conditions other than major depression. The fact that Prozac's side effects are more tolerable encouraged its prescription for other symptoms, including some that had been considered the exclusive province of psychotherapy. These have included excessive sensitivity to criticism, fear of rejection, lack of self-esteem, and a deficiency in the ability to experience pleasure. When people with these complaints sought professional help in the past, they turned to a psychological treatment—ranging from psychoanalysis and psychodynamic psychotherapy to cognitive-behavioral therapy and group therapy. But now, many patients with these complaints respond, often dramatically, to Prozac.

The major messenger of the news about Prozac is Peter Kramer, a psychiatrist whose earlier practice had focused on psychotherapy and who has also written extensively about psychotherapy both as columnist in a trade publication, *Psychiatric Times*, and as the author of a popular book. Now Kramer has written a best seller, *Listening to Prozac*, in which he reveals his enthusiasm for the use of this drug to transform people's behavior more efficiently and, often, far more effectively than prolonged psychological treatment.

Attitudinal Changes in Psychiatry

The widespread prescription of Prozac and related SSRIs for problems other than major depression, and the public and professional interest in Kramer's book, signal a major attitudinal change in American psychiatry. For many years the theoretical basis of the field derived from the writings of Sigmund Freud and his successors who emphasized the importance of childhood experiences in the generation of psychopathology—and the importance of insight in its amelioration. Although the education of psychiatrists also included training in the management of the seriously mentally ill and, since the 1950s, the use of psychopharmacological agents, the soul of the field continued to be Freudian. Of course Freud repeatedly predicted a time when chemistry and biology would also fruitfully inform psychiatry. Kramer's conversion reflects the growing consensus among clinical psychiatrists that this time has come.

But Freud might have been disappointed to learn that clinical psychopharmacology, like psychoanalysis, is not yet based on a deep mechanistic understanding. It had, in fact, been Freud's hope that ultimately studies of synaptic function would lead to an understanding of psychopathology. Yet even today advances in clinical psychopharmacology have not come about by elegant deduction from an understanding of how the brain controls behavior but instead by chance discoveries based on fragments of information. The development of Prozac depended on the accidental discovery of the antidepressant effect of imipramine; the initial isolation of serotonin from blood serum; the finding that imipramine blocks serotonin's reuptake; and a trial-and-error search for SSRIs. This is science at an early stage, and such bits of knowledge could not have predicted the value of this drug for so much of psychiatry.

Nor do these bits of knowledge reveal the mechanism of Prozac's clinical effects. How, in fact, does an agent whose primary action is to block serotonin reuptake produce sustained and coherent effects on behavior? There are, after all, already 14 different serotonin receptors identified in the brain, many with distinctive distributions. Assuming that the duration of action of serotonin at all of these receptors is regulated by reuptake, Prozac would be expected to affect them all. How does that lead to a reduction in the despondence of the depressed, alleviate anxiety in the fearful, and change the outlook of those who are sensitive to rejection? Perhaps selectivity comes because Prozac, by blocking reuptake, only augments the action of serotonin at those brain synapses where it is already being released. Does it, in this way, selectively strengthen already ongoing restorative mechanisms?

The problem is even more complicated, because the therapeutic effect of Prozac depends on adaptive changes in the brain that apparently take weeks to develop. This is suggested by the lag of up to a month before Prozac, imipramine, or many other chemically distinct antidepressants (including those that are selective norepinephrine reuptake inhibitors) become effective. Presumably their primary actions in prolonging neurotransmitter effects set into motion a series of molecular changes in the brain that may mitigate depression, alleviate anxiety, or alter temperament. But are these different psychological phenomena all alternative manifestations of the same underlying problem? Or are different adaptive changes put in motion in different underlying disorders? Explaining this chain of events is the most challenging current problem in psychopharmacology.

Clinical Questions Remain

There are pressing clinical problems as well. Are the personality changes reported by Kramer and other clinicians really due to Prozac's pharmacological effects, or is the drug just an expensive placebo? Are the effects attributable solely to the drug or rather to its combination with some form of psychotherapy? Are the changes lasting? Must the drug be taken forever? Controlled clinical trials are needed, but both the critical therapeutic variables and the behavioral changes may be subtle and difficult to measure. And, since pharmaceutical companies are often reluctant to test such secondary applications, financial support for work of changes may be subtle and difficult to obtain. Yet there is a critical need to formally evaluate what are for now only persuasive, but unverified, clinical impressions about Prozac's efficacy.

But most important is the impact of these developments on the overall field of psychiatry. When chlorpromazine and imipramine were first introduced, they were initially popular only with a small subgroup of psychiatrists who called themselves biological psychiatrists and who tended to focus on serious mental illness, leaving other more common and less severe problems to those who specialized in psychotherapy. Now it is becoming generally appreciated that modern psychopharmacology, genetics, and other offshoots of biology are also relevant to an understanding of the less serious behavioral disorders. The fact that new enthusiasts for this position include Kramer and many others who had viewed themselves as being primarily psychotherapists signals a shift in the intellectual main-stream of this field. Whether Prozac ultimately proves to be of value in altering rejection sensitivity or low self-esteem, the new openness to biological treatment will have profound effects on the way we educate the next generation of psychiatrists and on our ability to attract the interest of biological scientists in psychiatric problems. In thinking about Prozac, we have been led to reevaluate our basic assumptions about behavioral disorders and how we approach them.

Looking Back on the First Decade of Prozac and Other New Antidepressants

Nancy Wartik

The Food and Drug Administration approved the use of Prozac (fluoxetine) in the United States in late 1987. In the following selection, first published in 1996, health writer Nancy Wartik looks back on the first decade since the introduction of Prozac—a time that also saw the introduction of similar antidepressants such as Paxil (paroxetine) and Zoloft (sertraline). Wartik surveys developments in the use of Prozac and notes how the new class of antidepressants has reshaped society's views of depression. She states that Prozac has been both praised as a miracle cure and vilified as a "happy pill" that causes its users to ignore or mask underlying psychological reasons for their depression. People have also claimed that Prozac sometimes causes bizarre and violent behavior—claims that Wartik argues have not been substantiated by research. She concludes that the drug, while not effective for all who have tried it, has been an overall boon both for many depressed patients and for American society.

Five years ago, a traumatic sexual encounter sent Cindy Thompson,* now 41, plummeting into depression. "It was agonizing," recalls

**Names have been changed.*

Thompson, a public relations consultant in Baltimore. "I wanted to kill myself every day." Thompson's psychotherapist recommended Prozac. "But I resisted," she says. "I was concerned about using a chemical to alter my mind and emotions." Finally, poised between the knife drawer and the telephone, "I called my therapist." Thompson agreed to be briefly hospitalized—and to try Prozac. "I figured I'd hit bottom and had nothing left to lose."

This year [1996] marks a decade since Prozac, the antidepressant that's achieved a celebrity normally associated with movie stars and rock groups, first hit the market. Since then, it's been glorified as a miracle cure and vilified in a backlash centering on claims that Prozac makes some users violent. It's also been attacked as a "happy pill," a quick fix that allows users to ignore the psychological issues at the root of their depression. Yet even with its luster tarnished, Prozac prospers. With 1995 sales topping $2 billion, up 24% from 1994, it's the second biggest moneymaking drug in the U.S., after the ulcer medicine Zantac. According to the manufacturer, Eli Lilly, more than 14 million Americans have joined the Prozac generation.

The drug has touched the lives of women in particular, primarily because they're twice as likely as men to suffer from major depression—a partly genetic disorder marked by persistent symptoms including sadness, fatigue, sleep or appetite problems and suicidal thoughts. Women also tend to have higher rates of other disorders for which Prozac is now prescribed, such as dysthymia (chronic mild depression), some forms of anxiety (panic attacks and obsessive-compulsive disorder), severe PMS and bulimia.

Has the advent of Prozac been a boon for women, or will it come to be seen as the 1990s equivalent of "Mother's Little Helper"? Has the drug transformed the treatment of mental illness, or will it cause as yet unknown health problems down the line? Such questions are all the more pressing in this era of managed care, when there's a growing tendency to treat psychological disorders with medication rather than prolonged (read: pricey) talk therapy. And with a host of newer antidepressant clones such as Zoloft, Paxil and Serzone flooding the market, should Prozac still reign as the drug of choice? Ten years into the Prozac phenomenon, we're starting to get some answers.

A Revolution in Treatment

Antidepressants work by altering balances of mood-regulating chemicals, such as serotonin, in the brain. The most popular antidepressants used to be a class of drug known as tricyclics, which were developed in the 1950s and are still in use. But tricyclics affect not only the brain chemicals they're supposed to but also some they aren't. This can lead to side effects ranging from constipation, dizziness and weight gain to more dangerous problems such as heart rhythm abnormalities.

In contrast, Prozac, Paxil and Zoloft, which belong to a class of drugs known as selective serotonin reuptake inhibitors, or SSRI's, affect serotonin regulation much more directly, which means users tolerate them better. "It doesn't matter how well a drug works if, because of the side effects, people don't take it regularly," says Michael Norden, M.D., a psychiatrist at the University of Washington in Seattle and author of *Beyond Prozac*. "So Prozac was a tremendous step forward."

Women in particular seem to find Prozac and the other SSRI's easy to tolerate. In an ongoing multicenter study of people with chronic depression, women and men were randomly assigned to tricyclic or SSRI treatment. More than 25% of the women on tricyclics stopped taking them, largely because of the side effects, while less than 15% of women on SSRI's quit. They also reported better moods while using SSRI's. (Men, on the other hand, tended to do better on tricyclics.)

With findings such as these, it comes as no surprise that antidepressants are now prescribed more liberally than ever. Some 60% are given out by family doctors, rather than mental health specialists. They're also prescribed for a far greater range of ailments and for less serious disorders: Whereas tricyclics were once reserved only for those with severe depression, these days it's not uncommon for physicians to prescribe Prozac for a case of the blues.

Happy All the Time?

Prozac's easy accessibility has also raised fears that doctors are handing out the drug like M&M's and people are popping it for "personality face-lifts." The real story is more complicated. Plenty of experts agree that the drugs are too readily available. "Their popularity has led to some inappropriate use," says Sidney Zisook, M.D., a professor of psychiatry at the University of California at San Diego. "There are a lot of sloppy diagnoses, cases where they're given for the wrong reasons or for too long. There are also patients who just want to be perfect, to always enjoy themselves, and they think they can do it the easy way, with Prozac. But it's wrong to use these medicines to try to solve all of life's problems."

Others point to a tendency, encouraged by managed care, for doctors to prescribe a pill instead of steering patients toward psychotherapy. "There are maybe 20% to 30% of depressed patients who can just take a drug and get well," says New York University psychiatrist Eric Peselow, M.D. "But the majority need psychotherapy as part of treatment. Racing to Prozac isn't the only answer." Unfortunately people who pop a pill without doing the hard work of self-examination may find themselves back where they started when they quit taking the medication.

Yet with only one in three depressed people today getting treatment, cries of "Prozac abuse!" can be misleading. "There are far more people who could benefit from these drugs and aren't taking them than there are people taking them inappropriately," says Dr. Zisook. Prozac's trendiness shouldn't obscure the fact that the drug and its progeny help many people dramatically.

Despite her initial skepticism, for instance, Thompson

found the drug "life transforming. I felt like myself again."
Prozac also pulled Isabel Leigh up from despair. Leigh, 41, a
New York City editor who has struggled with depression on
and off for years, was reluctant to try the drug. "I didn't want
to be just one more trendy Prozac taker," she says. "I told myself it was a crutch I could do without." But about a year ago
she found herself feeling lethargic, hopeless and unable to
concentrate; she withdrew from friends and let work slide. Finally Leigh went to a doctor and got a Prozac prescription. "It
took a few weeks, but the difference was incredible," she says.
"I realized I'd been trying to overcome a biochemical problem
with willpower alone."

Prozac Pitfalls

Glowing testimonials aside, Prozac isn't perfect. Like any currently available antidepressant, it works in only 60% to 70%
of cases. There's often a lag of up to eight weeks before the
drug starts working. And Prozac isn't free of side effects either:
Potential problems include agitation, insomnia, headache and
weight gain or loss. What's more, perhaps a third of those who
stay on Prozac for nine months or more find that its uplifting
effects fade away, a problem ingloriously known as "Prozac
poopout." (Increasing the dose once or twice often helps.)

A growing number of studies also show that up to half of
all Prozac users experience decreased libido and delayed or no
orgasm. Sharon Keene, 39, a writer in Laguna Hills, CA, took
Prozac for three months and "it seemed to help in just about
every way," she says. "But I ended up stopping, because I
couldn't achieve orgasm. If I wasn't married, maybe I wouldn't
have cared so much, but it was affecting my relationship with
my husband."

Though other SSRI's can impair sexual function too, Zoloft
and Paxil leave the bloodstream faster than Prozac, so users
may be able to circumvent trouble in bed by taking drug "hol-
idays" a day or two before the act (so much for spontaneity).

Serzone, on the market since 1995, is kinder to users' sex lives. So is Wellbutrin, a medication with a slightly different mechanism of action than Serzone and the SSRI's. It does add a very slight risk of seizures, though. . . .

The bottom line: None of the new antidepressants is clearly superior. "They all have advantages and disadvantages," says Dr. Zisook. "We never know with certainty which drug will work best. There's always some trial and error involved."

The Price of Fame

As the leader of the pack, Prozac is often the drug of choice by benefit of name recognition alone. But its fame works against it too. Even today Prozac's reputation is clouded by rumors it can't quite shake. Within two years of its introduction in the U.S., headlines and lawsuits began claiming that Prozac drives some users to bizarre, violent behavior. One notorious 1989 incident, the subject of a new book called *The Power to Harm* by John Cornwell, involved a 47-year-old printing plant worker who shot 20 coworkers and then committed suicide after being on Prozac. Survivors and relatives of the victims sued Eli Lilly and lost, but the damage to Prozac's reputation was done.

Today you can surf the Net and still find horror stories from disgruntled folks in "Prozac survivor" support groups. Mary Beth Mrozek, a 33-year-old Buffalo, NY, mother of three who has bipolar illness, says that while on the drug she hallucinated, became convinced people were plotting against her and violently attacked loved ones. "I was a totally different person," she says.

Should the average Prozac user worry about having a Jekyll and Hyde reaction? Bipolar patients who take Prozac may be at slightly higher risk for an episode of mania. But that's a risk associated with any antidepressant (though possibly less so with Wellbutrin). Based on a substantial body of research, experts agree that Prozac users overall aren't at greater risk for violent or suicidal behavior. In fact, says Dr. Norden, "Depressed people who avoid Prozac are probably placing themselves in greater danger. Nothing increases suicide risk as much as depression itself."

A Cancer Connection?

Perhaps a more realistic worry involves unknowns about the long-term effects of Prozac and the other SSRI's, especially since some users are now staying on the drugs indefinitely. A slender body of evidence, based mostly on animal and very preliminary human studies, suggests that antidepressants, including Prozac, could accelerate tumor growth in some people who have a predisposition to cancer or preexisting tumors. Not surprisingly, Eli Lilly disputes these findings. "Lilly's long-term animal studies have been extensively reviewed by the FDA," says Freda Lewis-Hall, M.D., a psychiatrist who heads the Lilly Center for Women's Health in Indianapolis. "There is absolutely no scientifically credible evidence that it either causes or promotes cancer."

Not everyone agrees. Oncologist Lorne Brandes, M.D., of the Manitoba Cancer Treatment and Research Foundation in Winnipeg, Canada, questions how carefully Lilly interpreted some of its data. But at the same time, he says that antidepressants are "absolutely warranted to treat depression. I'd just suggest trying to get off them as soon as you comfortably can."

Ultimately, however, we may remember Prozac not for its side effects, trendiness or even its effectiveness, but for the attention it has focused on depression—and that can only benefit women in the end. "Once, to be depressed was to be morally and spiritually weak," says Dr. Zisook. "Now people in line at the grocery store are talking about being on Prozac. The drug has brought depression out of the closet."

Leigh, for one, is grateful that it did. "It's not like I have a perfect life with Prozac," she says. "I still have ups and downs. But now I know that if I do get down, I'll come back up. Before Prozac, I was never sure."

CHAPTER THREE

Recent Developments and Controversies Surrounding Antidepressants

Americans Turn to Natural Antidepressants

Somlynn Rorie

While Prozac and similar antidepressants continued to soar in popularity in the 1990s, many people remained dissatisfied with them and the side effects they cause and turned to alternative medicines. In the following selection Somlynn Rorie describes some of the nutritional supplements and herbal medicines that many Americans have tried to treat their depression, including amino acids, a chemical compound called SAM-e, and herbs such as St. John's wort and ginkgo biloba. Such alternative medicines can be just as effective as synthetic antidepressants and have fewer side effects, she claims. Rorie is a writer and editor for *Health Supplement Retailer*, a dietary supplement industry magazine that is distributed to health food stores.

Depression is a common illness that strikes about one in 15 Americans each year. It is the number one complaint heard by primary-care physicians, according to Richard Brown, M.D., author of *Stop Depression Now*, and more than 50 percent of the American population suffers from moderate depression at least once in a lifetime.

Rather than just "getting over it," men and women who are depressed often require treatment of the illness. According to the National Institute of Mental Health, symptoms of depression may include a persistent sad or empty feeling; a loss of energy and appetite; and a lack of interest in socializing, work or hobbies. Depression can come in various forms ranging from mild to moderate or severe. Mild depression is characterized by difficulty in maintaining normal activities; moderate depression may involve impaired functioning at work or in social activities; and severe depression, which may involve delusions or hallucinations, markedly interferes with a person's ability to function normally and may lead to suicide. Genetic factors may put a person at greater risk for developing depression, and alcohol or drug use can make symptoms worse.

Current biochemical theories of depression suggest that biogenic amines may play a significant role in depression. This group of chemical compounds transmits nerve impulses across a synapse—a junction where nerve impulses pass to a neuron or another cell. Amines such as norepinephrine, serotonin and, to a lesser extent, dopamine, acetylcholine and epinephrine have been extensively studied for their roles in the pathophysiology of depression. Serotonin, in particular, has been the subject of intense research for the past 25 years.

Antidepressant medications affecting these amines include monoamine oxidase (MAO) inhibitors, tricyclic antidepressants and selective serotonin inhibitors (SSRI). MAO inhibitors increase norepinephrine levels, SSRIs block serotonin inactivation, and tricyclics enhance norepinephrine transmission. Psychotherapies combined with conventional antidepressant drugs such as Prozac and Paxil have become more widely used in the past several years and have been found to be effective remedies. However, patients have reported unpleasant side effects such as dry mouth, nausea, headache, or impaired sexual function or sleep. Because of these side effects, many patients have turned to natural treatments such as amino acid supplementation and herbal phytomedicines as an aid in treating mild depression. Popular choices include 5-hydroxytryptophan (5-HTP), SAM-e, St. John's wort, kava kava and ginkgo biloba. Researchers continue to study the benefits of these products and suggest that natural alternatives may provide fewer or less severe side effects than most conventional antidepressant drugs.

Amino Acids and Other Precursors

Amino Acids can act as neurotransmitters or precursors to other neurotransmitters such as serotonin. Supplementing with amino acids can ease symptoms of depression. Amino acids and related compounds used in the treatment of depression include L-tryptophan, L-tyrosine, L-phenylalanine and 5-HTP. Other players such as melatonin and SAM-e have also been suggested as effective antidepressant therapies.

 THE HISTORY OF DRUGS

Comparing St. John's Wort with Synthetic Antidepressants

To summarize the benefits of St. John's wort when compared with synthetic antidepressants:

• Its side effects are not nearly as severe, and far less frequent.

• It does not have adverse effects when mixed with alcohol.

• It is non-addictive.

• It does not produce withdrawal symptoms when you stop taking it.

• It does not produce habituation, or the need for increased dosages to maintain its effects.

• Its use can easily be restarted without requiring a long buildup period.

• It enhances sleep and dreaming.

• It does not produce daytime sedation. In fact, it has shown experimentally to enhance alertness and driving reaction time.

• It does not produce agitation or instability.

Hyla Cass, *St. John's Wort: Nature's Blues Buster*. Garden City Park, NY: Avery Publishing Group, 1998.

- L-tyrosine: A precursor to norepinephrine; may be valuable to the people who do not respond to most antidepressant drugs except amphetamines.
- L-phenylalanine: Converted to tyrosine (a naturally occuring form of phenylalanine); D-phenylalanine (which does not normally occur in the body or in food) is metabolized to phenylethylamine (PEA), an amphetamine-like compound that occurs normally in the human brain and has been shown to have mood elevating effects. Studies have shown that depressed people commonly have low levels of phenylethylamine.
- 5-HTP: A close relative to tryptophan and a part of the metabolic pathway that leads to serotonin production. Studies from around the world have found that 5-HTP has true antidepressant properties.
- SAM-e: A chemical compound found in all living cells; SAM-e can be found in more than 40 biomedical processes in the body. Supplementing the diet with SAM-e in depressed patients can result in increased levels of serotonin, dopamine and phosphatides, improve binding of neurotransmitters to receptor sites and increase serotonin and dopamine activity. The key to SAM-e's effectiveness is its ability to make brain cells more responsive to neurotransmitters such as serotonin and dopamine.

Phytomedicines

Phytomedicines such as St. John's wort, kava kava and ginkgo biloba may also have compounds that can aid in treating depression. Phytomedicines cannot only serve as weak MAO inhibitors but can also help alleviate specific symptoms of depression. According to Harold H. Bloomfield, M.D., author of *Healing Anxiety with Herbs* (1998), anxiety and depression frequently occur in tandem. "Irritability, difficulty concentrating, indecision, guilt, fatigue, sleep and eating disturbances, and chronic aches and pains are symptoms common to both disorders," said Bloomfield. In addition, almost half of the people who suffer repeated panic attacks develop a major case of depression, which can be attributed to low levels of serotonin found in individuals who suffer from either anxiety disorders or depression. With this in mind, herbs such as kava and ginkgo, which have been proven to help with anxiety, may also help in treatment of depression.

- St. John's wort: Researchers have discovered that this herb works like an SSRI (a class of antidepressant medication) and a weak MAO inhibitor. Numerous studies have confirmed that St. John's wort does possess antidepressive effects in cases of mild to moderate depression.

- Kava kava: Has soothing and stress-relieving qualities; studies have shown its effectiveness in treating anxiety and depression.

- Ginkgo biloba: Improves blood flow through the brain, accounting for its use as an aid in mental acuity. Appears to normalize neurotransmitter levels; a potent antioxidant that protects nervous system cells and regulates blood platelet stickiness. Studies have shown that ginkgo biloba may be used to improve mood and may be useful in conjunction with standard antidepressants to enhance effectiveness in patients who are resistant to standard drug therapies. Another study showed ginkgo's effectiveness in decreasing sexual dysfunction problems caused by antidepressant drugs.

St. John's Wort Is Not an Effective Treatment for Severe Depression

Debra Goldschmidt

Researchers in Europe have found the herb St. John's wort to be an effective treatment against mild and moderate depression, but their studies have been criticized for being too small and therefore inconclusive. Because of the growing popularity of St. John's wort in the United States, the National Institutes of Health (NIH) decided to sponsor clinical trials of the herb's effectiveness. The results of the second clinical trial—the largest to date at that time—were announced in April 2002. The following selection by Debra Goldschmidt describes the results of that trial and people's reactions. Researchers concluded that St. John's wort was no more effective than a placebo. Furthermore, the lead researcher stated that the evidence indicated that St. John's wort should not be given as a treatment for major depression. However, critics of the study say it is irrelevant because St. John's wort is not billed as a treatment for severe depression but is effective in treating mild to moderate depression. Goldschmidt is a producer and assignment editor for *CNN Medical News*.

St. John's Wort, a popular herbal supplement, is not effective in treating cases of depression, according to a study released [April 9, 2002].

The study drew immediate fire from supporters of the supplement, who said it is effective in treating mild and moderate cases of depression.

The over-the-counter supplement is widely used to treat depression—in many cases by patients who don't consult doctors.

The Study

In the largest clinical trial to date on the supplement, researchers at Duke University Medical Center measured the effectiveness of the supplement by comparing a group of patients using St. John's Wort to patients being treated with a placebo.

The researchers also looked at a control group of patients being treated with the antidepressant sertraline (sold as Zoloft).

The 340 patients, unaware of which treatment they were receiving, were given a dosage three times a day for eight weeks.

The patients were assessed weekly or biweekly and those that responded, at least partially, during the first eight weeks were entered into an 18-week continuation phase.

After eight weeks, improvement was cited in 32 percent of patients treated with a placebo, versus 24 percent of those taking St. John's Wort, according to the study.

Such improvement was cited in 25 percent of those treated with Zoloft, but Dr. Jonathan Davidson—the lead researcher—cautioned that the Zoloft was administered in lower than the normal clinical dose, which could account for its relatively low success rate.

The findings were published in the *Journal of the American Medical Association*. It was the second study within a year to question the effectiveness of St. John's Wort.

"Major depression is treatable, but this research suggests that major depression of at least moderate severity should not be treated with St. John's Wort," Davidson said.

Other clinical trials have found St. John's Wort to be as effective as conventional antidepressants in treating mild to moderate depression, according to the National Center for Complementary and Alternative Medicine, part of the National Institutes of Health.

And Davidson said St. John's Wort could prove effective for people who suffer from milder forms of depression, noting his study looked only at major depression characterized as moderately severe.

Questioning the Study

Patrick Bridges, vice president of marketing for Abkit Inc.—the U.S. distributor for one of the makers of St. John's Wort—called the study "inappropriate."

"The study isn't relevant," Bridges said, pointing out that the supplement is not billed as a treatment for major depression, but is effective in cases of mild to moderate depression.

Davidson said that rather than using over-the-counter treatments, "patients are strongly advised to consult an appropriate health care provider to assess the best treatment for a depressive episode."

He said he believes the popularity of St. John's Wort is because it is so available. Davidson cautioned that just because a product is "natural" does not mean that it is safe.

St. John's Wort has been shown to interact dangerously with medications such as those taken to prevent rejection from organ donation, those used to treat some cardiac conditions, and medications for HIV and AIDS.

According to the National Institute of Mental Health, major depression affects approximately 9.9 million American adults age 18 and older in any given year and is a leading cause of disability in the United States.

In 1998, U.S. sales of St. John's Wort were estimated to be $210 million, according to a previous Duke University study.

The current [April 2002] study was funded by the National Center for Complementary and Alternative Medicine, the National Institute of Mental Health and the Office of Dietary Supplements. All three are divisions within the National Institutes of Health.

Zoloft

The inclusion of the Zoloft control group was to provide a cross-check of the study's validity rather than to test that medication's effectiveness, according to the report.

A spokesman for Pfizer, the maker of Zoloft, said that while the company was happy with the way the study was conducted, it had 10 years of clinical studies that proved the drug worked.

Studies of Zoloft are typically "flexible dosage trials," in which a patient's dosage is adjusted to achieve maximum clinical benefit. The control group in this study was given a set dosage.

Antidepressants Cause People to Be Violent

Rob Waters

In May 1998 television comedian and actor Phil Hartman was shot and killed by his wife, Brynn, who then killed herself. Early news accounts suggested that Brynn's shocking act might have been the result of a cocaine addiction relapse. In May 1999, however, a wrongful death lawsuit was filed by lawyers for the Hartmans' estate and children against the drug company Pfizer, blaming the antidepressant Zoloft for Brynn's actions.

In the following selection journalist Rob Waters writes that Zoloft and other antidepressants have been blamed for many violent actions and deaths besides the Phil Hartman tragedy. Lawyers and drug-industry critics have argued that antidepressants can cause such violence by creating a condition called akathisia, in which people experience extreme agitation, anger, and frustration. But Waters also notes that drug manufacturers have vigorously disputed the claim that antidepressants can provoke homicidal and suicidal acts. Waters is a freelance journalist whose articles have appeared in *Health*, *Parenting*, and the *Los Angeles Times*. He is the coauthor of *From Boys to Men: A Woman's Guide to the Health of Husbands, Partners, Sons, Fathers, and Brothers*.

It was May 1998, and comedian Phil Hartman and his wife, Brynn, were planning a party. Their son, Sean, was soon turning 10 and they wanted to make it special with a bash at Planet Hollywood. Brynn was inviting her son's friends, including some of his classmates from his school in Encino.

In mid-May she called Kathryn Alice, the mother of one of Sean's friends, to get her address. Sean and Calvin, Kathryn's son, played together and had visited each other's homes. Through their sons, the moms had gotten to know each other, too. They chatted on the phone, and Brynn confided that things were tough. "She said she was barely hanging on by a thread," Alice recalls. "I told her things will get better, but she said 'I don't know.'"

The invitation soon arrived in the mail, but the birthday party never happened. On May 28, at about 2:30 A.M., Brynn Hartman returned home from a night out with a female friend. As Sean and his sister, Birgen, slept in their rooms, Brynn entered the master bedroom and shot her sleeping husband three times. Four hours later, with police in the house and friends listening outside, Brynn lay down on the bed next to Phil's body and pulled the trigger once more, killing herself.

How could this happen? Why did a woman who was, by all accounts, a devoted and protective mother, deprive her children of their parents? In the days after the killings, the tabloids and mainstream press ruminated over the problems in the couple's often stormy relationship, speculating that Phil was preparing to leave her, or that she had relapsed into an old cocaine addiction. *People* magazine reported that she had recently started drinking again after 10 years of near-sobriety and had checked into an Arizona rehab clinic earlier in the year. Indeed, toxicology reports cited in press accounts indicate that at the time she died, Brynn Hartman had both cocaine and alcohol in her system.

But the couple's family and their lawyers have another answer: Zoloft made her do it.

In late May 1999, one year after the deaths, attorneys for

the Hartmans' estate and children filed a lawsuit against Pfizer, the pharmaceutical giant that makes Zoloft, a new-generation antidepressant similar to Prozac. The suit contends that Brynn Hartman's violent outburst was caused by a rare but previously documented side effect of the medication that left her agitated, jittery and "out of touch with reality." It is one of more than 170 wrongful death lawsuits filed against the makers of these new antidepressants since Prozac first hit the market 12 years ago.

The Hartman suit also charges that Arthur Sorosky, the psychiatrist that supplied Brynn Hartman with Zoloft, was not really her doctor and never conducted an evaluation. Sorosky, the complaint alleges, was actually her son Sean's doctor and gave Brynn medication samples—the kind doled out to physicians by drug company salesmen—"without the benefit of a history and physical examination [or] diagnosis."

Sorosky's attorney, Joel Douglas, told *Salon Health* that his client and Brynn Hartman had "a doctor-patient relationship" and that Sorosky had prescribed the Zoloft in a proper and appropriate way. "From what I understand," he added, "with cocaine and alcohol in her system, you don't need to look for Zoloft to understand what happened."

Blamed for Violent Deaths

But Zoloft and Prozac—along with other similar antidepressants—are being blamed for hundreds of violent deaths, including these:

- July 1997: Thirteen-year-old Matthew Miller of Overland Park, Kan., kills himself in his closet one week after he begins taking Zoloft. According to his father, Mark Miller, Matthew had been moody and withdrawn for about nine months—the result, Miller believes, of the family moving to a new neighborhood and Matthew starting at a new school. In June, his parents took him to a psychiatrist. The doctor, accompanied by two medical students in training, talked with Matthew and his parents, but Matthew had little to say. When they met again three weeks later, one thing Matthew did tell him—in response to a question—was that he would never consider suicide. The doctor ruled out attention deficit disorder, but offered no other diagnosis to the Millers. But he did give them a three-week supply of Zoloft to try, and told them to check back in a week. Seven days later, members of Matthew's family noticed that he seemed agitated. That night, he took his own life.

- Feb. 19, 1997: Patricia Williamson, 60, of Beaumont, Texas, stabs and slashes herself more than 100 times in the bathtub while her husband eats breakfast in their kitchen. On the advice of a psychiatrist, she had begun taking Prozac six days earlier to help her through a depression that had arisen just a few months before. Her husband, hearing strange noises in the bathroom, pried open the door and found his wife of 20 years semi-conscious in a pool of her own blood. She died the next day in the hospital. Lawyers for Eli Lilly, the pharmaceutical giant that makes Prozac, recently reached an out-of-court settlement in the case.

- March 1996: Daryl Dempsay, 35, stabs his wife and two children at their home in Burlington, Kan., then shoots and kills himself with a .22-caliber rifle. His wife and children survive, and have charged in a recently filed suit against Pfizer that Dempsay's violent outburst was caused by an adverse reaction to Zoloft, which he had been taking for several weeks.

What would cause these people to become so violent or suicidal? The surviving family members and their lawyers—along with some experts and anti-psychiatry activists—contend that this volatile behavior is an extreme manifestation of a rare side effect of the new antidepressants.

The side effect, called akathisia, creates a feeling of distress, agitation and restlessness that leaves people jittery and unable to sit still or to stop shaking their legs. "In its milder form," wrote Pfizer scientist Roger Lane in a journal article published last year [1998], "it is experienced as a vague feeling of appre-hension, irritability, dysphoria, impatience or general unease."

"Akathisia is like being tortured from within," says Peter Breggin, a Maryland psychiatrist and prominent critic of Prozac and other psychiatric medications. "It's like the screeching of chalk down a board, only it's going down your spinal column.

"This agitation or akathisia drives a person into extreme states of irritability, anger, and frustration," Breggin continues. "People can become more depressed and more despairing; their impulse control loosens and they do stupid things. So the violent impulses that an ordinary person would control come pouring out or even appear for the first time."

In his article, Pfizer's researcher Lane described the suicide risk of SSRIs—selective serotonin reuptake inhibitors, the class of drug to which Prozac and Zoloft belong—in this way: "It may be less of a question of patients experiencing . . . suicidal ideation, than patients feeling that 'death is a welcome result' when the acutely discomforting symptoms of akathisia are ex-perienced on top of already distressing disorders."

Lane's article focused specifically on akathisia and other sim-ilar side effects caused by SSRIs. Yet the word "akathisia" never appears in the package insert for Zoloft that is supposed to in-form doctors about the risks and side effects of medication. And while akathisia is mentioned as a rare side-effect in the Prozac insert, both companies continue to publicly underplay the risks.

"This is an old story, it's gone around and around," says Jeff Newton, a spokesman for Eli Lilly. "But there's ample evi-dence that Prozac is in no way linked to these kinds of violent behavior." In fact, he added, Prozac reduces aggressive behav-ior and may lower the risk of suicide.

Clashing Views on Antidepressants

Pfizer representative Celeste Torello rejected the notion that Zoloft had any role in causing suicides or violence. "There's no scientific or medical evidence that Zoloft causes violent or suicidal behavior," she told *Salon Health.* "At this point, there have been over 90 million prescriptions written and there hasn't been any evidence that it causes anything close to what Brynn Hartman did." (When asked why Roger Lane, her own company's scientist, discussed akathisia in his journal article but the company included no similar information in their package inserts, she declined to comment due to the pending lawsuit.)

To Andy Vickery, the lead attorney in the Hartman case and the other cases mentioned above, the failure of Pfizer and Eli Lilly to adequately warn doctors and patients about the possible risks constitutes gross negligence. "They withhold critical information from prescribing physicians, the public and the patients," he says—information that would help doctors and patients recognize the symptoms of akathisia in time to do something about them.

Eli Lilly's contention that Prozac is safe is bolstered by two jury verdicts in the company's favor—one several years ago in a Louisville, Ky., case and the other earlier this year [1999] in Hawaii. In the Hawaii case, a jury cleared the drug maker in the death of a Hawaii man who killed himself and his wife 10 days after he began taking Prozac. (However, a motion for a new trial was heard on July 1, due to complaints by two jurors that they did not actually concur with the supposedly unanimous verdict. A ruling is expected shortly.)

"Litigation [against Lilly] has never worked," Newton claims, though he acknowledges that Lilly has settled some lawsuits out of court. Newton claims the number is "very small" and they were made strictly as a business decision to avoid tying up company scientists and lawyers. Vickery says he settled nine Lilly cases last year alone, and has several more pending or waiting to be filed.

Not a New Issue

The idea that SSRIs can trigger suicidal or homicidal behavior is far from new. Indeed, the issue first exploded into public consciousness 10 years ago, when a former employee of a Louisville printing plant, Joseph Wesbecker, strolled into the plant with an AK-47 and started shooting. He killed eight people, wounded 12 and then turned the gun on himself. Wesbecker had been taking Prozac for about a month, a fact seized upon by attorneys for the shooting victims and trumpeted on TV talk shows. Wesbecker's sons did *Larry King Live;* one of the surviving victims went on the Donahue show for a program called "Prozac: the medication that makes you kill." They claimed that Wesbecker had never been violent prior to taking Prozac.

But that claim was disputed by accounts in the local newspapers, which portrayed Wesbecker as a man with a deeply troubled past who had been hospitalized for mental disorders on three occasions, had made numerous suicide attempts and had reportedly told his wife a year before his rampage that he'd like to go to the plant "and shoot a bunch of people."

About the time of the Louisville shooting, Harvard psychiatrists were finishing up an article for the *American Journal of Psychiatry* about six patients who "developed intense violent suicidal preoccupation" after taking Prozac for two to seven weeks. While three of the patients had attempted suicide in the past as a result of their depression, none were suicidal at the time they started on Prozac, the authors reported, and none had experienced suicidal urges on other psychiatric drugs. For all of them, their fixation with dying abated after they stopped taking the drug.

The article, coauthored by a leading expert on psychiatric drugs, sparked great interest and controversy within the psychiatric and pharmaceutical world. Other clinicians soon weighed in. A series of journal articles reported on cases in which patients on Prozac developed akathisia. When they stopped taking the medications, the researchers reported, the violent or suicidal urges abated.

Eli Lilly itself disputed the validity of case reports involving individual patients, criticizing them as inferior to the randomized clinical trials the firm had sponsored involving thousands of patients. Those studies, the company claimed, showed no evidence of suicidal impulses emerging among patients taking Prozac. Other researchers agreed with Eli Lilly, and submitted their own studies that found no increased suicide risk from Prozac.

In 1991, the FDA joined the fray, assembling a panel of experts to study the issue of Prozac and suicide and report back. The panel's conclusion: There was no credible evidence linking the drug to acts of suicide or violence.

Though critics complained that the panel had been stacked with paid consultants to Eli Lilly, its opinion—coupled with Eli Lilly's success in dismissing or settling out of court scores of lawsuits—seemed to settle the issue and remove it from the public spotlight. Until now [1999].

School Shootings

Now the Hartman case and two violent school shootings committed by teenagers on antidepressants have pushed the issue back into the headlines. Eric Harris, one of the teenage gunmen at Columbine High in Littleton, Colo., was taking the antidepressant Luvox to treat obsessive-compulsive disorder. Kip Kinkle, the 15-year-old Illinois boy who killed his parents and two classmates last year before trying to take his own life, was reportedly on Prozac.

These two sensational cases, trotted out by critics of psychiatry like Breggin and columnist Arianna Huffington may, in fact, be poor examples. Kip Kinkle was reportedly obsessed with guns long before he started taking Prozac nearly two years before his rampage. And Eric Harris' carnage, far from an act of drug-addled rage, had been meticulously planned for months.

And then there was Brynn Hartman. Given the cocaine and alcohol in her system, could any jury be made to believe that Zoloft was responsible, rather than the booze or the drugs? Perhaps there was a terrible interaction between all three substances—the Zoloft package label does warn that the drug should not be taken in conjunction with alcohol. It does not specifically mention cocaine, though common sense suggests that combining the drugs would not be the smartest idea. The lawyers for the Hartman family will try to make the case that Brynn's behavior changed during the two weeks or so during which she took the Zoloft, immediately prior to the killings. They argue in the complaint that her symptoms started several days before the shootings. She was having trouble sleeping, the suit claims, and complained that she felt "weird," telling her nanny that she was having adverse effects from the drug. She told one friend that she was "going to jump out of her skin" and the friend advised her to talk to Sorosky. The lawsuit claims that on May 24, four days before her death, she called him and told him about her reaction to the drug. His advice, according to the complaint: Cut the dosage in half.

When Kathryn Alice turned on her TV and learned of the Hartman deaths, she was stunned. "I never saw a sign of her being that off-balance," she says. "She had a real strong instinct to protect her children. She was very involved with her kids and very concerned—constantly setting up play dates and picking them up and dropping them off. She was a really good mother."

Antidepressants May Cause Teen Suicide

Marilyn Elias

Prozac is the only SSRI antidepressant that has been approved by the Food and Drug Administration (FDA) for people under the age of eighteen. However, many psychiatrists and general medical practitioners prescribe their child and teen patients other antidepressants that have been tested and specifically approved only for adults—a practice that is perfectly legal. According to the FDA, 2.7 million children under twelve and 8.1 million adolescents took antidepressants in 2002.

Some people are concerned that antidepressants may cause some teens to commit suicide. In December 2003 a British government health agency advised doctors not to prescribe seven popular antidepressants to children (Prozac was excluded from the warning) because their benefits did not outweigh the possible increased risk of suicide. The FDA in 2004 began an official review of clinical studies of antidepressants to determine if they pose risks to children that warrant banning their use for young populations. In March of that year, the FDA began to require that the makers of ten antidepressants put labels on their bottles to warn doctors and parents about their possible dangers for children. The following article by Marilyn Elias, a journalist for *USA Today*, describes some of the ongoing legal and regulatory developments and some of the tragic stories of young people who committed suicide while on antidepressants.

Could antidepressants prescribed for more than 1 million U.S. children and teenagers cause some of them to attempt suicide?

The Food and Drug Administration's first public hearing on this question Feb. 2 [2004] is expected to draw polarized and emotional testimony. But the evidence needed for an answer won't be in for several months, says Russell Katz, director of the FDA's neuropharmacological division.

Reviewing the Data

The FDA is re-examining 20 studies of eight antidepressants used in children. The studies didn't document a single drug-related suicide. But preliminary findings suggested that suicidal thoughts and attempts, though rare, were more common in kids taking the drugs than those on sugar pills.

Now the FDA is checking to make sure that children on antidepressants weren't more suicide-prone to start with than the placebo group and that the suicide attempts were bona fide tries. "Right now the data are quite murky," Katz says.

The FDA has asked drug companies for more information. The review may find no link between the drugs and suicidal thoughts, or a problem with some but not all antidepressants. The analysis also may find qualities—for example age, sex or length of illness—that put certain kids at higher risk, he says.

The newer antidepressants in question, called SSRIs or SSNIs, make "feel good" chemicals more available in the brain and were viewed as safe.

Now the FDA and many parents are concerned. The agency has cautioned doctors about possible risks, and in December [2003] Britain's equivalent of the FDA advised giving none of the SSRIs to children except for Prozac, saying it's the only one whose benefits outweigh risks.

Prozac also is the sole SSRI approved by the FDA for treating depressed kids 7 to 17, but others, such as Zoloft and Celexa, can be prescribed legally "off label" since they're approved for adults.

Some scientific experts think the worry is unwarranted. Research shows that SSRI antidepressants don't increase suicidal behavior in kids, says a preliminary report . . . from the Amer-

 THE HISTORY OF DRUGS

Weighing the Research

What is known about the effects of some leading antidepressants on kids. *

DRUG AND MAKER	COMMENT
Zoloft Pfizer	Two studies show Zoloft significantly improved depression in 69% of patients, versus 59% taking a placebo.
Prozac Eli Lilly and generic, called fluoxetine	In one study, 41% of kids taking the drug showed a complete remission of depression, compared with 20% taking a placebo. In January [2003] the FDA approved Prozac for use in children 7 to 17.
Paxil GlaxoSmithKline	One study found 63% of kids taking the drug showed improvement versus 46% taking a placebo, but the drug was ineffective in two other studies. The FDA is evaluating reports of increased risk of suicidal thinking and attempts in kids who use it. Both the FDA and British authorities recommend children under 18 not take it.
Celexa Forest Laboratories	In an unpublished study, 36% of kids taking Celexa showed improvement, compared with 24% taking a placebo.

* Studies vary in methodology and how they measure improvement.

"Antidepressant Use for Kids Gains Support," *Wall Street Journal*, August 27, 2003.

ican College of Neuropsychopharmacology. Depression, not the drugs, is probably causing suicide attempts, the scientists say.

There's relatively little controlled research on SSRIs in school-age children "and zippo on kids under 5," says John March, chief of child and adolescent psychiatry at Duke University Medical Center in Durham, N.C.

Soaring Usage

But national surveys suggest soaring usage among kids, up about 60% from the mid-90s to 2000. More than 1 million children and teens now receive SSRI prescriptions, estimates Julie Magno Zito, a psychiatric drug expert at the University of Maryland.

"The lack of supporting data, considering their widespread use, is surprising and disturbing," says Lawrence Diller, a behavioral pediatrician in Walnut Creek, Calif., and author of *Should I Medicate My Child?*

Still, many therapists say SSRIs can help kids, and untreated depression isn't benign. Major depression raises the risk of childhood suicide about twelvefold, according to federal figures. Every survey finds that most depressed kids get no treatment.

But does it have to be drugs? March, who has studied SSRIs, thinks not. Cognitive-behavioral therapy, which teaches kids to change self-defeating attitudes and behaviors, is about as effective as Prozac, "and that should be tried first," he says; drugs should be reserved for the most severely depressed, who need therapy, too.

Children on SSRIs must be monitored closely, says David Fassler, a child psychiatrist in Burlington, Vt. Although most kids have no problems on the medications, the SSRIs can spark agitation and impulsive acts, perhaps leading to suicide attempts, Fassler and other experts speculate.

However, prescribing patterns and medical economics work against the eagle-eye monitoring needed, some say. General practitioners and pediatricians, often not experts in the field, write the majority of SSRI prescriptions for kids. Also, HMOs may restrict access to busy specialists and pay for pills but not therapy, Fassler says.

Warning Signs

Even specialists may prescribe incorrect doses of poorly studied drugs or fail to inform parents about warning signs. Mark Miller, 54, of Overland Park, Kan., believes antidepressants cost the life of his 13-year-old son, Matthew. He'll testify at the [February 2004] FDA hearing.

After a family move in 1996, Matthew had trouble adjusting at his new school. On the advice of school counselors, the Millers took him to a psychiatrist the next summer, though he seemed happier.

The doctor gave Matthew antidepressants, and he began to act fidgety, Miller says. The morning after Matthew took his seventh pill, Mark's mom found him hanging by a belt from a laundry hook in his closet.

"We have no family history of depression and didn't even have a package insert because he gave us samples," Miller says. An autopsy showed his son's body had SSRI levels suitable for a 250-pound body, though the boy weighed less than 100 pounds, he says.

But other parents will tell the FDA that SSRIs saved their kids' lives.

Sherri Walton, 45, of Paradise Valley, Ariz., says major depression runs in her family. Walton's daughters, Jordan, 14, and Katie, 12, started Prozac in the past 18 months after episodes of severe depression.

"They didn't even want to dance anymore, even though they're avid dancers; they didn't want to live, and now they're normal kids," Walton says. "I'm going to tell the FDA, 'Don't take away what gave my kids their lives back.'"

The agency expects to have enough evidence to answer the

questions on suicide risk by summer [of 2004], the FDA's Katz says. Another hearing is likely then, and at that time the FDA might issue a new recommendation on SSRIs and children.

Parents who want their kids off the antidepressants now should consult doctors on how to do it gradually because stopping abruptly can be harmful, he adds.

Doctors Believe Depression Can Be Cured with Antidepressants

Hara Marano

Hara Marano is editor at large of the monthly magazine *Psychology Today* and edits the journal's *Blues Buster* newsletter. In the following selection she describes the state of depression treatment fifteen years after the introduction of Prozac in late 1987. She argues that Prozac and similar antidepressants have changed how psychiatrists and doctors treat depression. They are no longer trying simply to manage the disease but to cure it altogether. Part of the challenge they face is convincing patients to try one or more antidepressants for long enough periods of time to effect a cure regardless of the side effects.

Fifteen years ago [1987], Prozac launched a revolution. It rendered depression a disorder that was—finally—safely treatable. The torrent of prose hailing Prozac and its chemical kin eventually made the mental illness dinner-party discourse. Today, a much quieter revolution in treatment is taking place. It, too, has its origins in Prozac and its siblings, the selective serotonin reuptake inhibitors.

Fifteen years of experience with reasonably safe treatments has given the mental health world a new understanding of the

Hara Marano, "How to Take an Antidepressant," *Psychology Today*, January/February 2003. Copyright © 2003 by Sussex Publishers. Reproduced by permission.

disorder and its true course: It's no longer enough to merely treat depression; it's necessary to banish it.

Increasingly, the aim of treatment is not to make patients better but to make them completely well. In the absence of full remission from an episode of depression, the disorder tends to recur. What's more, studies now show that the longer patients remain sick, the harder it is for them to recover completely.

"It became very clear over the past several years that people who don't achieve full remission are at high risk for relapse and for doing poorly," says Jonathan Alpert, M.D., Ph.D., associate director of the depression research program at Massachusetts General Hospital in Boston. "Even if they don't have a full relapse, they don't do well in social and occupational function."

There is no magic bullet; evidence indicates that the available antidepressants are equally effective. All of the drugs get 70 percent of people better within six to ten weeks, according to David Dunner, M.D., director of the Center for Anxiety and Depression at the University of Washington. However, "better" does not necessarily mean symptom-free. "There isn't any difference among the drugs regarding that."

Where the drugs do differ, however, is in the side effects they create, especially in the long haul. Side effects have become a central consideration in the new approach to depression treatment.

Long-term treatment is also critical. Data indicate that individuals should be treated for at least nine months following their first acute episode. If they have chronic depression—an episode lasting two years or more—they need to be treated for two years after remission. "And if they have recurrent depression marked by multiple episodes, perhaps forever," notes Dunner.

However, the average duration of a prescription is about 100 days. "It's a serious problem," Dunner points out. "We're not treating people nearly long enough."

Nor is treatment aggressive enough, according to Alpert: "Really pushing for remission may mean using two antidepressants at once or pushing the dose up higher than one would normally use."

Pick Your Pill

For many experts, the most sensible approach to selecting an antidepressant is to factor in the presence of associated or co-occurring conditions. Anxiety disorders, for example, commonly accompany depression. The selective serotonin reuptake inhibitors (SSRIs) have been well studied for the major anxiety disorders: panic, social phobia, generalized anxiety

THE HISTORY OF DRUGS

The Gifts of Depression

Miriam Greenspan, a writer and practicing psychotherapist, argues in this selection from her book Healing Through the Dark Emotions *that people must confront and work through their feelings of depression and despair rather than rely on antidepressants to conform to cultural standards of cheerfulness.*

What I've noticed is that, before Prozac, people didn't expect to feel better so fast. Now they do. Prozac has lowered our affect tolerance for despair (no doubt to the delight of the pharmaceutical behemoths). Before Prozac, people in my practice felt better within four to six months by journeying through despair and healing their souls. Now there is less patience for this kind of time frame. . . .

The judicious use of antidepressants where it's a matter of life and death is one thing. No one wants to feel bad all the time, and it is by no means a moral failing to use the new antidepressants if one chooses to do so. But helping people "fit" into the culture and preserving the cultural status quo is hardly the endgame of psychotherapy, or at least it shouldn't be. It contributes little to our nation's mental health and only guarantees continued mental health problems. Our hyperthymic culture disorder and obsessive-compulsive disorder.

"For someone who has depression and social phobia, it's reasonable to use a medication whose effectiveness has been well documented for both disorders," reports Alpert. The data also suggest that SSRIs are "reasonable first choices" for those with eating disorders.

But antidepressants don't work if people don't take them. Patients have to be willing to put up with side effects that range from drowsiness to seizures. As true as that is for short-term treatment, it's even more the case with long-term treatment. "The issue is, what can we do to get these patients to

has a dark underbelly that, in many respects, is the ground of the current epidemic of despair we call depression. Depression, paradoxically, takes root in a soil that is antagonistic to despair. The ways in which conventional psychology has become a force for conformist individualism have been roundly criticized by many, and justly so.

Moreover, beyond helping them "fit in," what can we offer to those who carry despair for the culture? Women, the elderly, the disenfranchised, and artists, among the most vulnerable to despair, might have something to contribute to the culture from out of their despair, rather than in spite of it. What gifts lie in these darker realms? And what about confronting the denied darkness of our culture and society?

This is where listening to Prozac just doesn't cut it. . . .

I'm not opposed to the wise use of antidepressants, but doing so in a medical model, in the absence of any validation for the emotion itself, can make despair's journey seem like an absurd exercise in anguish to no end. Discovering the value of despair demands a great deal of internal work and patience. Listening to despair is difficult. . . .

And yet, listening to despair can have a fertile richness that cannot be found in a capsule.

Miriam Greenspan, *Healing Through the Dark Emotions*. Boston: Shambhala, 2003.

stay on the drugs for the length of time the evidence now suggests is best?" explains Dunner.

In the long run, two side effects are especially bothersome: sexual dysfunction and weight gain. The SSRIs are strongly linked to sexual dysfunction in both sexes—diminished libido, erectile dysfunction and delayed, attenuated or absent orgasm. In one recent study, up to 70 percent of patients receiving the newer antidepressants reported sexual dysfunction when asked directly about it. That contradicts the 15 percent declared on product labels. Some of the atypical antidepressants—such as Wellbutrin (buproprion) and Remeron (mirtazapine)—do better at preserving sexual function.

In regard to weight gain, the SSRI antidepressants do not appear to be created equally. Paxil, for one, seems to cause more problems. One study, by Andrew Nierenberg, M.D., associate director at Massachusetts General's clinical depression and research program, showed that after six months, patients put on more weight with Paxil than with the other antidepressants. Evidence favors non-SSRIs for avoiding weight gain, particularly bupropion and Serzone (nefazodone). Nefazadone, however, bears a Food and Drug Administration warning that it can cause liver failure in rare instances.

Paxil also causes more sexual dysfunction, which leads many individuals to discontinue their regimen. Teresa* found that Paxil stanched her anxiety and depression after only two weeks. "I was calmer. My emotions weren't erupting," recalls the 55-year-old social worker. But the flip side was a sense of muted emotions and diminished sexual appetite. "The libido isn't just your sex drive, it's your passion for life," say Teresa. She plans to continue taking Paxil despite the side effects. "It did what I wanted it to do, which is take away the pain."

Psychiatrists believe that side effects are a matter of negotiation. "Some of the most teary exchanges in my office have involved women who don't want to gain weight on a drug,"

*Names have been changed.

confides John Herman, M.D., director of clinical services in psychiatry at Mass General. "The patients come in tearful because they're depressed; then they come in no longer depressed but distraught because they are way overweight."

"It's a stealth side effect," observes Jerrold Rosenbaum, M.D., chief of psychiatry at Massachusetts General. "It emerges subtly over time and surprises everybody."

Physicians must consider what is tolerable in exchange for a medication's primary effects and understand that the bar has been raised. "As the cookie lady Mrs. Fields once said, 'Good enough is not good enough,'" says Dunner. "Just because a patient improves doesn't mean the treatment should be stopped."

Sometimes the problem lies with patients themselves. Often, they feel better and stop their medication, thinking it's no longer needed. "Although an individual patient might win, it's a mistake," observes Dunner. "The odds are against her."

At least as often, side effects interfere with long-term patient compliance. Therefore, clinicians must know how to manage the dosage or try to augment the antidepressant with another medication so the patient will stay on course. Psychostimulants such as Dexedrine, Ritalin and Adderall are widely used as antidepressant adjuncts, even though their primary indication is for attention deficit disorders or narcolepsy. Provigil, recently approved for the treatment of narcolepsy, is also used to boost the efficacy of antidepressants or reduce the drowsiness they cause. Thyroid hormones and natural remedies such as omega-3 fatty acids and SAM-e are also being explored.

Leading psychopharmacologists contend that antidepressant treatment can be delivered in a way that instills confidence in patients—enough to ride out early difficulties. "I try to emphasize the early side effects that might occur and how to manage them," reports Dunner. "So if a patient suffers from them, he doesn't say, 'What is all this about?'"

It's also important for patients to know that taking one pill will not instantly make them better; in fact, the drugs are not likely to begin working for three to four weeks. Treatment will then progress in eight to twelve weeks.

Some 30 percent of depressed patients do not respond to the first drug they try. If there is no improvement after a patient uses a medication at an adequate dose and for an adequate duration of time, a switch is in order. A drug with a different mechanism of action may be preferred. The trial, though, isn't lost. The patient may have lost time, but valuable information has been gained.

"We're trying to get the patient over that last little hump," says Dunner. "Granted, we can improve most patients, but can we actually get them back to normal? I think we can do this with many more patients than we used to."

Marketing Paxil as a Cure for Shyness

Shankar Vedantam

As antidepressant use became more widespread in the 1990s, makers of these drugs sought to promote their use to alleviate problems other than clinical depression. The following selection by *Washington Post* staff writer Shankar Vedantam describes how one pharmaceutical corporation sought to expand sales of its product by publicizing the existence of a heretofore little-known malady called social anxiety disorder. In 1999 GlaxoSmithKline, the company that makes the antidepressant Paxil, began an extensive public relations and marketing campaign that included arranged appearances by psychiatrists on television and radio shows, assistance to nonprofit advocacy organizations, and advertising directed at doctors and potential patients. The marketing campaign greatly increased sales of Paxil, which was at that time the only FDA-approved medication for social anxiety disorder. But it raised questions among some mental health experts who question whether social anxiety disorder is a legitimate disease and who fear that people with simple shyness may be encouraged to take unnecessary medication. Shankar Vedantam is a journalist and a playwright.

About two years ago [in 1999], newspaper, magazine and television news stories began popping up across the country about a little-known malady called social anxiety disorder. Psychiatrists and patient advocates appeared on television shows and in articles explaining that the debilitating form of bashfulness was extremely widespread but easily treatable.

The stories and appearances were part of a campaign, coordinated by a New York public relations agency, that included pitches to newspapers, radio and TV, satellite and Internet communications, and testimonials from advocates and doctors who said social anxiety was America's third most common mental disorder with more than 10 million sufferers.

So successful was the campaign that according to a marketing newsletter, media accounts of social anxiety rose from just 50 stories in 1997 and 1998 to more than 1 billion references in 1999 alone. And about 96 percent of the stories, said the report in PR News, "delivered the key message, 'Paxil is the first and only FDA-approved medication for the treatment of social anxiety disorder.'"

The plug for a drug was no accident. Cohn & Wolfe, the public relations agency coordinating the campaign, did not serve at the pleasure of the doctors and patient advocates who participated in the education campaign. Instead, the agency worked at the behest of SmithKline Beecham, the pharmaceutical giant now known as GlaxoSmithKline, which makes the antidepressant Paxil.

The campaign was supplemented by a multimillion-dollar marketing and advertising blitz that pitched the drug to doctors, audiences of television shows such as "Ally McBeal" and readers of magazines such as *Rolling Stone*. Sales of Paxil, which had been lagging those of Prozac and Zoloft, jumped, rising 18 percent [in 2000] alone.

The education and advertising campaigns have raised concerns that pharmaceutical companies, traditionally in the business of finding new drugs for existing disorders, are increasingly in the business of seeking new disorders for existing drugs. Critics accuse the companies of recruiting patients by teaming up with doctors and patient advocates—with all the attendant conflicts of agenda and conflicts of interest.

"Pharmaceutical companies who are marketing psychopharmacological treatments have gotten into the business of selling psychiatric illness," says Carl Elliott, a bioethicist at the University of Minnesota, who studies the philosophy of psychiatry. "The way to sell drugs is to sell psychiatric illness. If you are Paxil and you are the only manufacturer who has the drug for social anxiety disorder, it's in your interest to broaden the category as far as possible and make the borders as fuzzy as possible."

Blurring the line between normal personality variation and real psychiatric conditions can trivialize serious mental illness, some experts say.

"Some marketing seems to imply that huge proportions of the population need pharmaceutical intervention for relatively common problems, and in the long run, I am concerned that that may undermine the credibility of the concept of serious mental illness," says Rex Cowdry, medical director of the National Alliance for the Mentally Ill, a patient advocacy group.

GlaxoSmithKline did not make company officials available for comment, despite repeated requests. But doctors and advocates associated with the company's campaign defend the effort, saying it informed thousands of people who previously did not know they were suffering from the disorder, spurring many to seek needed help.

"When I talk to family physicians, I don't hear them saying I have all these people who are asking for medicines they don't need," says Murray Stein, a psychiatry professor at the University of California in San Diego. "They say this patient said she had social anxiety and I've been treating her for years and I never thought to ask about it. What could be negative about that?"

Although many of the participants say they served as paid consultants or scientific investigators for the company, they reject any notion that they were manipulated by the pharmaceutical industry. Most say they had spent years toiling on social anxiety disorder and were delighted when SmithKline offered a way to get their message out.

"I know there's lots of concern about, 'Are we medicalizing normative things and is the pharmaceutical industry trying to put SSRIs in the water,'" Stein says, referring to the class of drugs known as selective serotonin reuptake inhibitors, which includes Paxil. "The people I see talking about that have not seen these patients."

Advocacy Groups and Public Relations Firms

Patients with social anxiety disorder aren't the shy people who hang out at the edges of parties. Those truly suffering from the condition are profoundly debilitated, refusing promotions or taking jobs as night guards because they can't stand to be around people. Some cannot open the door to a handyman because that would mean conversation.

"Would somebody who is not having problems take a medicine that is costly and has side effects?" Stein asks. "I don't think too many people would do that. The idea that this is cosmetic psychopharmacology I find offensive."

The advocacy organizations that participated in the campaign—the American Psychiatric Association, the Anxiety Disorders Association of America and a Long Island–based group called Freedom From Fear—say that the only way for nonprofit groups to get out a potent public health message is to team up with a pharmaceutical company with deep pockets. Moreover, the groups demanded and received full control over the editorial content of the education campaign, says John Blamthin, an APA spokesman.

"We have never, ever promoted any drug," says Jerilyn Ross, the founder of the Anxiety Disorders Association of America. "If you look at our materials and on our Web site, we have never mentioned a drug." Ross says that she even got into "fights" with SmithKline because she frequently told the company's marketers, "'We can't do this, we can't do that.'"

But if the experts did not want to be boosters for Paxil, the arrangement with the public relations firm—and the marketing campaign for Paxil, which offered journalists interviews with some of the same experts—made that confusing. Cohn & Wolfe emphasized in its calls to the media that it spoke on behalf of doctors and nonprofits—not the pharmaceutical company that was paying its bills.

The Cohn & Wolfe Web site, however, made no secret of the fact that it is in the business of marketing, not public health: On a previous campaign to promote coverage about the 10th anniversary of Prozac's launch in Britain, the agency said it successfully helped drug maker Eli Lilly spin coverage. The strategy? Offer journalists interviews with "independent Key Opinion Leaders"—doctors, advocacy groups and patients with "suitable 'positive-Prozac'" experiences, "thereby distancing Lilly from a potentially negative debate."

Cohn & Wolfe declined to talk about its role in the Paxil campaign, calling the information "proprietary and confidential."

Marcia Angell, a former editor of the *New England Journal of Medicine*, says that pharmaceutical companies could not be expected to act solely in the interest of public health: "They are no more in the business of educating the public than a beer company is in the business of educating people about alcoholism."

The expensive ad and education campaign paid off in the crowded antidepressant market: GlaxoSmithKline's 2000 annual report told shareholders the drug "became number one in the U.S. selective serotonin reuptake inhibitor market for new retail prescriptions in 2000."

Barry Brand, Paxil's product director, told the journal *Advertising Age*, "Every marketer's dream is to find an unidentified or unknown market and develop it. That's what we were able to do with social anxiety disorder."

The Ethics of Marketing

Several experts, including some who treat social anxiety disorder, worry whether such marketing is in the public's best interest.

"When the pharmaceutical companies focus on broadening the market, you miss out on the fact that there is a proportion of people for whom mental illnesses are truly disabling," says Cowdry, who formerly headed the National Institute of Mental Health. "I have the same reaction when I hear that one in three Americans have a mental illness. The problem with that kind of data is that it undermines credibility—it doesn't pass the laugh test."

Two experts who were assembled by the American Psychiatric Association to write the definition of social anxiety disorder for the psychiatrist's manual say they admire the campaign for alerting patients suffering in silence. Still, they have concerns.

"I don't think the ads make the distinction between social anxiety and shyness," says Edna Foa, a professor of psychology at the University of Pennsylvania who served on the APA committee. "One gets the impression from the ads that if you are shy and you have some difficulties and you want to be outgoing, then take Paxil. You are promoting medication when it is unnecessary."

There were other instances where the social anxiety marketing campaign diverted from the message of medical experts—including experts who were part of the education campaign—or quoted the experts selectively.

The campaign said that more than 10 million Americans suffered from social anxiety disorder, making it the most common mental disorder after depression and alcoholism—and that 13 percent of Americans are affected by social anxiety disorder. But the National Institute of Mental Health says only about 3.7 percent of the U.S. population has social anxiety disorder. The American Psychiatric Association says rates vary between 3 percent and 13 percent. Stein of UCSD says he prefers the 3 percent to 4 percent estimate.

Although Paxil has been specifically approved by the Food and Drug Administration for the disorder, many psychiatrists say there is probably little difference between Paxil and similar medicines such as Prozac or Zoloft in treating social anxiety. There are also other types of drugs available for treating other forms of anxiety.

And although the campaign mentioned a psychological therapy called cognitive behavior therapy, it did not stress that the therapy is as effective as medication, has no side effects, such as sexual problems and fatigue, and does not require patients to stay on treatment indefinitely.

"In my opinion, social anxiety is not a chemical problem with the brain," says Jonathan Abramowitz, a psychologist at the Mayo Clinic in Rochester, Minn., who worked on the psychiatrist's manual. "I see it as a problem with normal thinking and behaviors that have gone awry."

Cognitive behavior therapy, he says, takes 14 weeks: "It's like learning to ride a bike. You are practicing these skills over and over. No one can take them away from you the rest of your life. The long-term benefits of cognitive therapy is better than medicine because with medicine, when you stop, the symptoms come back."

Repackaging Prozac for Women

Margot Magowan

In the late 1990s Eli Lilly and Company, the corporation that had made billions of dollars selling Prozac but whose patent on the drug was set to expire in 2001, created a pink and lavender version of the pill and named it Serafem. Eli Lilly heavily promoted Serafem to consumers and doctors as a treatment for premenstrual dysphoric disorder, a severe variant of premenstrual syndrome. Critics accused Eli Lilly of using questionable marketing tactics in an effort to preserve its sales once its patent had expired and generic brands of Prozac became available. The following selection by Margot Magowan provides one such critique. Magowan is a writer, radio-show producer, and founder of the Woodhull Institute, a nonprofit educational organization in San Francisco that provides leadership training and professional development for women.

The Pills are so pretty, so pink and lavender. Prozac, the controversial bad-boy drug of the '90s, had a makeover and a comeback. Now it has a kinder, gentler look and a new name: Serafem.

In case you couldn't tell by the color scheme, Serafem is marketed just for women—specifically, women in their late 20s and early 30s—to combat a condition known as Premenstrual Dysphoric Disorder, or PMDD. Symptoms are said to include depression, anxiety, anger and sensitivity to rejection. PMDD is called a more severe form of the collective symptoms known as premenstrual syndrome (PMS).

Though the federal Food and Drug Administration last July [2000] approved marketing Prozac as Serafem, psychiatrists disagree with the PMDD diagnosis and list the disorder as "needing further study."

I, for one, couldn't be happier that Eli Lilly—the company that created both Prozac and Serafem—has found a cure for sensitivity to rejection. I always found it a useless emotion. . . .

Lest you worry that a lot of head shrinks (amateurs included) will slow Eli Lilly's launch of Serafem, rest assured that the drug's debut is accompanied by a multi-million dollar media blitz. You can't miss it if you watch any TV.

One ad shows a woman struggling to untangle shopping carts at a supermarket.

Though she is visibly irritated, a voiceover consoles viewers that Serafem's pastel pills will restore her to the woman she really is.

The real woman—the one inside of this irritated shell of a woman—obviously does not get annoyed at the supermarket, an environment the female of the species ought to be able to navigate as easily as her own closet. A Stepford—sorry, Serafem—woman would never suggest to her partner in that irritated, you-know-she-hasn't-taken-her-medication-way, that he put down the remote control and do the shopping himself, while she relaxes in a bubble bath.

Going Out of Style

Why is Prozac making the shift from anti-depressant for the masses to a targeted girlie pill? It's because Prozac was about to go the way of grunge music, coffee bars and other has-beens of the '90s.

Prozac was going out of style.

When the drug came out 12 years ago [in December 1987], people popped it like Tic-Tacs. Best-selling books, such as Peter Kramer's "Listening to Prozac" and Elizabeth Wurtzel's

"Prozac Nation," were essentially positive about the drug—with Eli Lilly's trademarked brand name in their titles.

There was a national dialogue about Prozac. Was it right to take a pill to cure depression? Were we medicating human nature? How depressed did you have to be to take it? Had you taken it? Were you taking it now?

Alas, times have changed. Today [2001] Prozac is a victim of its own success, having spawned a whole family of two-syllable knock-offs—Buspar, Paxil, Zoloft.

Not only is Eli Lilly losing out to the competition, but more urgently, this summer Prozac's patent rights run out. The only way the company can prevent generic drug makers from flooding the market with cheaper, copycat versions, is to convince the FDA it has found a new use for Prozac.

Prozac sales were projected to fall from $2.51 billion in 2000 to $625 million in 2003.

So what's an aging, once-glamorous drug to do?

Find a new identity, a new image, a new wardrobe. Then get FDA approval and launch a publicity campaign. Enter Serafem, a drug with no past and no controversy.

Put it in spring colors! Give it a new name! Advertise to women!

Relaxed Restrictions on Advertising

Luckily for Prozac's new look, the FDA relaxed the regulations that kept prescription drug ads off TV. Now drug companies are allowed to take their glossy campaigns directly to the people. This way, patients go to the doctor's office humming jingles, listing their symptoms and asking for the desired drug by name. The doctor, once in the role of diagnostician, has evolved into the drug dispenser, the middleman between the drug company and you.

There are those who argue that identifying and diagnosing premenstrual conditions such as PMDD and PMS is pathologizing normal cycles and women's bodies in general. In support of this theory, statistics show neither condition exists in developing countries, implying PMDD is a culturally bound syndrome.

If this is correct, we would have to determine what conditions need to be changed to make the developed world a healthier place for women. Traits such as sensitivity to rejection would not be chalked up to hormone fluctuations, but as symptomatic of a culture where women are taught to be passive, don't learn to take risks and don't learn that failure is frequent and survivable.

Lest you forget, this is the same FDA that took 12 years to legalize RU-486, the abortion pill, but seems to have little trouble approving a pill that promises to keep women smiling at the supermarket.

The Next Wave of Antidepressants

Michael C. Miller

Michael C. Miller is assistant professor of psychiatry at Harvard Medical School and the editor of the *Harvard Mental Health Letter.* In the following selection he describes the latest theory on the cause of depression and the medical treatments researchers are developing to address this cause. Some research indicates that depression may not be caused by imbalances of serotonin and other brain chemicals as is commonly believed. Instead, depression may be caused by faulty nerve-cell connections in key parts of the brain. Miller predicts that the antidepressants commonly used today may be replaced with drugs that are able to manipulate one's emotional mood with greater control and precision.

In his 1968 novel "Do Androids Dream of Electric Sheep?" (which inspired the movie "Blade Runner"), Philip K. Dick introduced his hero fighting with his wife over what mood to be in. The couple, living in the dreary California of 2021, is fortunate enough to own a Penfield Mood Organ, a device that allows the user to dial up any desired state of mind. They spar over the wife's decision to schedule, twice a month, three hours of hopelessness and despair.

Would you want to manipulate your moods with such precision? If your hopelessness and despair were out of control, you probably would. As helpful as today's antidepressants are, about one third of depression sufferers get little or no relief from them. And because the causes of depression are still so poorly understood, it's hard to tell if an intervention is getting to the heart of the problem.

But the science is changing fast. Researchers are amassing new insights into the biology of depression. According to the new model, depression stems not from a "chemical imbalance" (too little serotonin, too little norepinephrine) but from unhealthy nerve-cell connections in the regions of the brain that create our emotions. If that's true—and the evidence is compelling—then the real goal of treatment is not to alter the brain's chemistry but to repair its blighted circuitry.

The new paradigm reflects a growing awareness of how chronic distress affects the brain. Our stress-hormone system, which kicks us into action in an emergency, may remain switched on in susceptible people, especially those who were very stressed during childhood. Overexposure to stress hormones slows the growth of nerve fibers in a region of the brain called the hippocampus. This brain center allows us to soak up sensory input, link experience to emotion and store all of it as coherent memories. The hippocampus is typically small in depressed people, with some brain cells lost and some shrunken.

The idea that depression is linked to stalled nerve-cell growth or faulty connections may explain an old mystery. If antidepressant medications boost neurotransmitter concentrations immediately (which they do), why does it often take six weeks or longer to feel better? Recent experiments in mice tell us that antidepressants stimulate the growth of new hippocampal nerve cells, which form connections with older nerve cells. This process takes several weeks. If drugs like Prozac ease depression by inadvertently boosting neurogenesis, the thinking goes, drugs designed specifically for that purpose might bring surer relief with fewer side effects.

That's a tall order, but researchers are already pursuing several strategies. One quest is to find a drug to block the action of Substance P, one of the chemical messengers involved in the stress response. Aprepitant, the first Substance P blocker to enter clinical trials, has recently proved worthless as an antidepressant. But other compounds are under study, and one of them may work.

A second possible target for therapy is CRH (corticotropin-releasing hormone), a chemical produced by the hypothalamus, a tiny part of the brain that integrates hormones with behavior. CRH starts a cascade that ends with the release into the bloodstream of the stress hormone cortisol. An experimental CRH blocker called R121919 can dampen the stress response, both in lab animals and in depressed patients, but it also damages the liver. Drug-makers are now developing other CRH blockers—and learning to manipulate still other parts of the stress response.

Drugs that suppress vasopressin—another hormone released under conditions of stress—leave rodents less anxious and more spirited. Drugs that mimic a stress-busting hormone called Neuropeptide Y have similar effects. They may also have the ability to reduce a mouse's desire for alcohol—pointing the way to a possible new biological model for alcoholism. Some experts believe these compounds are the next wave in antidepressants.

It may take us decades to understand the biology of depression. What we need in the meantime is as many unique treatments as we can get. We may not want a mood dialer as close at hand as the TV remote. But with any luck, these new ideas will soon deliver better ways to tune the only mood organ we have: the brain.

Facts About Antidepressants

- Antidepressants are medications used to combat the mental disorder of depression. They are available only by prescription and are generally taken under the supervision of a doctor or psychiatrist.

- Antidepressants alter the way brain chemicals called neurotransmitters work in the brain. Neurotransmitters, which include serotonin and noradrenaline, transmit signals between brain cells.

- According to the National Institute of Mental Health, in any given one-year period about 18.8 million American adults suffer from depression.

- Antidepressants are used to treat symptoms of depression such as sad mood, loss of appetite, sleep problems, feelings of hopelessness, guilt, lethargy, trouble concentrating, and preoccupation with death/suicide.

- Antidepressants are used not only to treat depression but also eating disorders, stress, anxiety and panic attacks, and obsessive-compulsive disorders.

- There are roughly thirty different types of prescription antidepressants available in today's market.

- Antidepressants are generally only part of the treatment for depression; they are often used in conjunction with psychotherapy and lifestyle changes.

- The benefits of taking antidepressants may not be noticeable until up to eight weeks of treatment.

- Some people stop taking antidepressants after six to twelve months; others use antidepressants as a long-term treatment to prevent more episodes of depression.

- Dosages of antidepressants vary according to a person's weight, age, and other factors. Patients generally begin on a low dose that is gradually increased as their depression symptoms are monitored by their doctors.

- Antidepressants should not be taken with other medications without consulting a doctor.

- Alcohol and street drugs may reduce the effectiveness of antidepressants. Antidepressants may increase the effects of alcohol, since both are metabolized by the liver.

- Antidepressants are not considered to be addictive like other drugs such as tranquilizers or nicotine, but some studies have shown that up to a third of people who quit taking them suffer from withdrawal symptoms such as dizziness, anxiety, and sensations in the body that feel like electric shocks.

- The effectiveness of some antidepressants can wear off in time (the phrase "Prozac poopout" refers to this phenomenon).

- Monoamine oxidase inhibitors (MAOIs) have been used since the 1950s and are effective for some people who do not respond to other types of antidepressants. They can interact dangerously with foods such as cheese; people on MAOIs must adhere to dietary restrictions.

- Tricyclics were the first line of chemical treatment for depression from the early 1960s to the late 1980s. Side effects of tricyclics may include dry mouth, a slight tremor, fast heartbeat, constipation, weight gain, and sexual dysfunction.

- Selective serotonin reuptake inhibitors (SSRIs) were introduced in the late 1980s beginning with Prozac in 1987 and became the most popular type of antidepressant in the 1990s. Side effects of SSRIs include sexual problems, headaches, nausea, nervousness, and agitation.

- The newest generation of antidepressants are SNRIs, which stands for serotonin and noradrenaline reuptake inhibitors. They were introduced in the late 1990s.

- Some people with depression have turned to herbal and alternative medications that are not FDA-approved and can be purchased over-the-counter. One popular alternative is St. John's wort (Hypericum perforatum).

- St. John's wort has been used for centuries to treat mental disorders and anxiety as well as for other medical uses, such as a balm for wounds.

- In Germany doctors recommend St. John's wort about twenty times more often than Prozac.

- The active ingredient(s) of St. John's wort remains unidentified, but some research suggests that the substance hyperforin may play a role in the herb's antidepressant effect.

- Reported side effects of St. John's wort include dry mouth, gastrointestinal upset, dizziness, fatigue, and increased sensitivity to sunlight.

- St. John's wort can interact with prescription drugs; individuals should consult with a health care professional before using it.

Table of Antidepressants

Monoamine Oxidase Inhibitors (MAOIs)

Chemical name	Trade name	Date introduced	Manufacturer
iproniazid	Marsilid	1958	
isocarboxazide	Marplan	1960s	Roche
phenelzine	Nardil	1960s	Parke-Davis
tranylcypromine	Parnate	1960s	GlaxoSmithKline

Tricyclics

Chemical name	Trade name	Date introduced	Manufacturer
amitriptyline	Elavil	1965	Merck
amoxapine	Asendin	1989	Watson
clomipramine	Anafranil	1990	Aventis-Pasteur
doxepin	Sinequan	1982	Pfizer
imipramine	Tofranil	1960	Novartis
maprotiline	Ludiomill	< 1982	Mylan
nortriptyline	Pamelor, Aventyl	1977	Eli Lilly
protriptyline	Vivactil	2000	Odyssey
trimipramine	Surmontil	< 1982	Wyeth-Ayerst

Selective Serotonin Reuptake Inhibitors (SSRIs)

Chemical name	Trade name	Date introduced	Manufacturer
citalopram	Celexa	1998	Forest
escitalopram	Lexa-Pro	2002	Forest Laboratories
fluoxetine	Prozac, Serafem	1987	Eli Lilly
fluvoxamine	Luvox	1994	Solvay
paroxetine	Paxil	1992	GlaxoSmithKline
sertraline	Zoloft	1993	Pfizer

Other

Chemical name	Trade name	Date introduced	Manufacturer
bupropion	Wellbutrin	1996	GlaxoSmithKline
mirtazapine	Remeron	1996	Organon
nefazodone	Serzone	1994	Bristol-Myers Squibb
trazodone	Desyrel	1982	Bristol-Myers Squibb
venlafaxine	Effexor	1997	Wyeth

1895

German psychiatrist Emil Kraepelin develops a classification of mental disorders, distinguishing between depression, bipolar disorder, and schizophrenia.

1900

Sigmund Freud publishes *The Interpretation of Dreams*, his seminal work on psychoanalysis.

1906

The Food and Drug Act is passed by Congress, putting the federal government in the business of regulating drugs and creating the Food and Drug Administration (FDA).

1938

The U.S. government passes the Federal Food, Drug, and Cosmetic Act, requiring evidence that drugs are safe before they can be put on the market.

1948

American scientists isolate serotonin, a brain chemical involved in memory and depression.

1952

Chlorpromazine (Thorazine) is used in the treatment of schizophrenia; its success motivates researchers to search for medications for other mental disorders, including depression.

1958

Iproniazid is introduced to the U.S. market as an antidepressant under the trade name of Marsalid. It is the first monoamine oxidase inhibitor (MAOI) to be used as an antidepressant.

1960

Imipramine is introduced in the United States under the trade name Tofranil. English scientists discover that antidepressants lower the levels of serotonin in the blood.

1962

Congress passes legislation giving the FDA power to withhold drugs from the market until the manufacturer can provide studies attesting to the drugs' effectiveness and safety.

1968
Swedish scientist Arvid Carlsson discovers that serotonin helps electrical impulses travel between brain cells and is subsequently reabsorbed by neurons; his discovery would lead to the development of Prozac and other SSRIs (selective serotonin reuptake inhibitors).

1972
Fluoxetine is developed by research scientists at Eli Lilly and Company.

1976
Clinical trials begin for fluoxetine.

1984
The German government approves the use of St. John's wort for depression and other mood disorders.

1987
Fluoxetine is approved for the U.S. market by the FDA and is introduced as Prozac.

1990
The Prozac Survivors Support Group, an organization of Prozac users and their relatives who have suffered from the drug's side effects, is established to warn people about the possible risks of the antidepressant.

1991
The FDA convenes a panel to look at the issue of whether antidepressants can cause suicidal thinking and behavior; they conclude that antidepressants are not to blame.

1992
Paroxetine (Paxil) is introduced to the U.S. market.

1993
Peter Kramer's book *Listening to Prozac* spends twenty-one weeks on the *New York Times* best-seller list. Sertraline (Zoloft) is introduced to the U.S. market.

1994

In the first lawsuit against Eli Lilly, the manufacturer of Prozac, a jury rules in favor of the defendant in a case involving a Kentucky man who killed several coworkers and then committed suicide after starting Prozac treatment. It was later revealed that the plaintiffs had reached a secret legal settlement with the corporation.

1996

Bupropion (Wellbutrin) is introduced to the U.S. market; it is one of the first new antidepressants that is not an SSRI.

1997

A study by Columbia University and the New York State Psychiatric Institute finds that the number of Americans treated for depression rose from 1.7 million in 1987 to 6.3 million in 1997. The number of prescriptions for antidepressants also doubled during that time.

2001

A jury blames Paxil for causing a man to kill his family and then commit suicide.

2002

New Mexico becomes the first state to pass legislation allowing licensed psychologists to prescribe antidepressants and other psychotropic medications. The National Center for Complementary and Alternative Medicine finds in a clinical trial that St. John's wort is no more effective than a placebo in treating depression.

2003

The FDA advises that antidepressant Paxil should not be prescribed to teens and younger children without further study. British medical regulators order doctors to stop prescribing several popular antidepressants, including Paxil, Zoloft, and Effexor, to children because of possible links to suicidal thoughts.

2004

The FDA holds public hearings on antidepressants to explore whether they lead children to commit suicide. The FDA directs antidepressant makers to include warning labels on their products stating that they cause some people to experience increased agitation, irritability, depression, and suicide risk.

ORGANIZATIONS TO CONTACT

The editors have compiled the following list of organizations concerned with the issues debated in this book. The descriptions are derived from materials provided by the organizations. All have publications or information available for interested readers. The list was compiled on the date of publication of the present volume; names, addresses, phone and fax numbers, and e-mail and Internet addresses may change. Be aware that many organizations take several weeks or longer to respond to inquiries, so allow as much time as possible.

American Academy of Child and Adolescent Psychiatry (AACAP)
3615 Wisconsin Ave. NW, Washington, DC 20016-3007
(202) 966-7300 • fax: (202) 966-2891
Web site: www.aacap.org

AACAP is a nonprofit organization that supports and advances child and adolescent psychiatry through research and the distribution of information. The academy's goal is to provide information that will remove the stigma associated with mental illnesses and assure proper treatment for children who suffer from mental or behavioral disorders. It publishes the monthly *Journal of the American Academy of Child and Adolescent Psychiatry* and fact sheets including "Psychiatric Medications for Children and Adolescents: Questions to Ask."

American Foundation for Suicide Prevention (AFSP)
120 Wall St., 22nd Fl., New York, NY 10005
(212) 363-6237 • fax (212) 363-3500
email: inquiry@afsp.org • Web site: www.afsp.org

Formerly known as the American Suicide Foundation, the American Foundation for Suicide Prevention supports scientific research on depression and suicide, educates the public and professionals on the recognition and treatment of depressed and suicidal individuals, and provides support programs for those coping with the loss of a loved one to suicide. It opposes the legalization of physician-assisted suicide. AFSP publishes a policy statement on physician-assisted suicide, the newsletter *Crisis*, and the quarterly *Lifesavers*.

American Psychiatric Association (APA)
1000 Wilson Blvd., Suite 1825, Arlington, VA 22209
(703) 907-7300
e-mail: apa@psych.org • Web site: www.psych.org

An organization of psychiatrists dedicated to studying the nature, treatment, and prevention of mental disorders, the APA helps create mental health policies, distributes information about psychiatry, and promotes psychiatric research and education. It publishes the *American Journal of Psychiatry* monthly and fact sheets on mental disorders including depression.

American Psychological Association (APA)
750 First St. NE, Washington, DC 20002-4242
(202) 336-5500 • fax: (202) 336-5708
e-mail: public.affairs@apa.org • Web site: www.apa.org

The American Psychological Association is the largest scientific and professional organization representing psychology in the United States and is the world's largest association of psychologists. It publishes numerous books, journals, and videos.

Canadian Mental Health Association (CMHA)
8 King St. East, Suite 810, Toronto, ON M5C 1B5 Canada
(416) 484-7750 • fax: (416) 484-4617
e-mail: national@cmha.ca • Web site: www.cmha.ca

The Canadian Mental Health Association is one of the oldest voluntary organizations in Canada. Its programs are designed to assist people suffering from mental illness find the help needed to cope with crises, regain confidence, and return to their communities, families, and jobs. It publishes books, reports, policy statements, and pamphlets.

Citizens Commission on Human Rights (CCHR)
6616 Sunset Blvd., Los Angeles, CA 90028
(800) 869-2247 • (323) 467-4242 • fax: (323) 467-3720
e-mail: humanrights@cchr.org • Web site: www.cchr.org

CCHR is a nonprofit organization whose goal is to expose and eradicate criminal acts and human rights abuses by psychiatry. The organization believes that psychiatric drugs, including some antidepressants, can cause serious mental health problems and violence. CCHR publishes numerous books, including *Psychiatry: Destroying Morals* and *Psychiatry: Education's Ruin*.

National Alliance for the Mentally Ill (NAMI)
Colonial Place Three
2107 Wilson Blvd., Suite 300, Arlington, VA 22201
(703) 524-7600 • fax: (703) 524-9094
Web site: www.nami.org

NAMI is a consumer advocacy and support organization composed largely of family members of people with severe mental illnesses such as schizophrenia, manic-depressive illness, and depression. The alliance adheres to the position that severe mental illnesses are biological brain diseases and that mentally ill people should not be blamed or stigmatized for their condition. Its publications include the bimonthly newsletter *NAMI Advocate* and the book *Breakthroughs in Antipsychotic Medications*.

National Foundation for Depressive Illness (NAFDI)
PO Box 2257, New York, NY 10116
(800) 239-1265
Web site: www.depression.org

NAFDI provides information about depression and manic-depressive illness. It promotes the view that these disorders are physical illnesses treatable with medication, and it believes that such medication should be made readily available to those who need it. The foundation publishes the quarterly newsletter *NAFDI News* and the fact sheet "Symptoms of Depression and Manic Depression."

National Institute of Mental Health (NIMH)
6001 Executive Blvd., Room 8184, MSC 9663, Bethesda, MD 20892-9663
(301) 443-4513 • fax: (301) 443-4279
e-mail: nimhinfo@nih.gov • Web site: www.nimh.nih.gov

NIMH is the federal agency concerned with mental health research. It plans and conducts a comprehensive program of research relating to the causes, prevention, diagnosis, and treatment of mental illnesses, including depression. It produces various informational publications on mental disorders and their treatment.

National Mental Health Association (NMHA)
2001 N. Beauregard St., 12th Fl., Alexandria, VA 22311
(800) 433-5959 • fax: (703) 684-5968
e-mail: nmhainfo@aol.com • Web site: www.nmha.org

NMHA is a consumer advocacy organization concerned with combating mental illness and improving mental health. It promotes research into the treatment and prevention of mental illness, monitors the quality of care provided to the mentally ill, and provides educational materials on mental illness and mental health. It publishes the monthly newsletter *The Bell* as well as books and pamphlets on understanding and overcoming mental illness.

Obsessive-Compulsive Foundation (OCF)
676 State St., New Haven, CT 06511
(203) 401-2070 • fax: (203) 401-2076
e-mail: info@ocfoundation.org • Web site: www.ocfoundation.org

OCF consists of individuals with obsessive-compulsive disorders (OCDs), their friends and families, and the professionals who treat them. It works to increase public awareness of and discover a cure for obsessive-compulsive disorders. It publishes the bimonthly *OCD Newsletter* and the pamphlet *OCD Questions and Answers.*

U.S. Food and Drug Administration (FDA)
5600 Fishers Ln., Rockville, MD 20857-0001
(888) 463-6332
Web site: www.fda.gov

As the agency of the U.S. government charged with protecting the health of the public against impure and unsafe foods, drugs, cosmetics, and other potential hazards, the FDA is the agency that approves the use of antidepressants and other prescription medications and issues public advisories about their use. It publishes the *FDA Consumer* magazine.

Books

Samuel H. Barondes, *Better than Prozac: Creating the Next Generation of Psychiatric Drugs.* New York: Oxford University Press, 2003.

Karen Bellenir, ed., *Mental Health Disorders Sourcebook: Basic Consumer Health Information About Anxiety Disorders, Depression, and Other Mood Disorders.* Detroit: Omnigraphics, 2000.

Peter R. Breggin, *The Anti-Depressant Fact Book: What Your Doctor Won't Tell You About Prozac, Zoloft, Paxil, Celexa, and Luvox.* Cambridge, MA: Perseus, 2001.

Peter R. Breggin and Ginger Ross Breggin, *Talking Back to Prozac: What Doctors Won't Tell You About Today's Most Controversial Drug.* New York: St. Martin's, 1994.

Hyla Cass, *St. John's Wort: Nature's Blues Buster.* Garden City Park, NY: Avery, 1998.

Debra Elfenbein, ed., *Living with Prozac and Other Selective Serotonin Reuptake Inhibitors: Personal Accounts of Life on Antidepressants.* San Francisco: HarperSanFransciso, 1995.

Joseph Glenmullen, *Prozac Backlash.* New York: Simon & Schuster, 2000.

David Healy, *The Antidepressant Era.* Cambridge, MA: Harvard University Press, 1999.

——, *Let Them Eat Prozac: The Unhealthy Relationship Between the Pharmaceutical Industry and Depression.* New York: New York University Press, 2004.

James Johnson and John D. Preston, *Clinical Psychopharmacology Made Ridiculously Simple.* Miami: Medmaster, 2001.

Peter D. Kramer, *Listening to Prozac.* New York: Viking, 1993.

Jonathan Michel Metzl, *Prozac on the Couch: Prescribing Gender in the Era of Wonder Drugs.* Durham, NC: Duke University Press, 2003.

Michael T. Murray, *Natural Alternatives to Prozac.* New York: Morrow, 1996.

Michael J. Nordeen, *Beyond Prozac: Brain-Toxic Lifestyles, Natural Antidotes, and New Generation Antidepressants.* New York: Regan, 1995.

Helen C. Packard, *Prozac: The Controversial Cure.* New York: Rosen, 1998.

Norman Rosenthal, *St. John's Wort: The Herbal Way to Feeling Good.* New York: HarperCollins, 1998.

Lauren Slater, *Prozac Diary.* New York: Random House, 1998.

Donna Smart, *The Shooting Drugs: Prozac and Its Generation Exposed on the Internet.* Payson, AZ: PRI, 2000.

Jean Thuillier, *Ten Years That Changed the Face of Mental Illness.* Malden, MA: Martin Dunitz, 1999.

Ann Blake Tracy, *Prozac: Panacea or Pandora?* West Jordan, UT: Cassia, 1994.

Carol A. Turkington, *The Hypericum Handbook: Using St. John's Wort, "Nature's Prozac," to Alleviate Depression.* New York: M. Evans, 1998.

Elliot S. Valenstein, *Blaming the Brain: The Truth About Drugs and Mental Health.* New York: Free, 2002.

Elizabeth Wurtzel, *Prozac Nation: Young and Depressed in America.* Boston: Houghton Mifflin, 1994.

Periodicals

Natalie Angier, "Drugs for Depression Multiply, and So Do the Hard Questions," *New York Times*, June 22, 1997.

Joseph Annibali, "Prozac on Trial," *World & I*, September 2000.

Sharon Begley, "One Pill Makes You Larger, and One Pill Makes You Small . . ." *Newsweek*, February 7, 1994.

Harold H. Bloomfield, "Treating Depression with Hypericum," *Saturday Evening Post*, November/December 1997.

Barry Brophy, "Kindergartners in the Prozac Nation," *U.S. News & World Report*, November 13, 1995.

Benedict Carey, "Youth, Meds, and Suicide," *Los Angeles Times*, February 2, 2004.

Michael Castleman, "Becoming Unblued," *Mother Jones*, May/June 1997.

Geoffrey Cowley, "The Culture of Prozac," *Newsweek*, February 7, 1994.

Greg Critser, "Oh, How Happy We Will Be," *Harper's Magazine*, June 1996.

Mary Crowley, "Do Kids Need Prozac?" *Newsweek*, October 20, 1997.

Richard DeGrandpre, "Trouble in Prozac Nation," *Nation*, January 5, 2004.

Hugh Drummond, "Of Medicines and Melancholy," *Mother Jones*, January 1987.

Economist, "Better than Well: Society's Moral Confusion over Drugs Is Neatly Illustrated by Its Differing Reactions to Prozac and Ecstasy," April 6, 1996.

Carl Elliott, "Pursued by Happiness and Beaten Senseless," *Hastings Center Report*, March/April 2000.

Deborah Franklin, "Treat Depression with More than Drugs," *Health*, April 1997.

Erica Goode, "Antidepressants Lift Clouds, but Lose 'Miracle Drug' Label," *New York Times*, June 30, 2002.

———, "Stronger Warning Is Urged on Antidepressants for Teenagers," *New York Times*, February 3, 2004.

Barbara Graham, "Meditating on Prozac," *Health*, September/October 1994.

Ginny Graves, "Getting Past Prozac (the Problems of Antidepressant Withdrawal)," *Harper's Bazaar*, May 2000.

Sanjay Gupta, "Been Down So Long . . . Prozac and Other New Drugs Triggered a Revolution in the Treatment of Depression. But Do We Still Need the Couch?" *Time*, January 21, 2002.

Gardiner Harris, "Debate Resumes on the Safety of Depression's Wonder Drugs," *New York Times*, August 7, 2003.

David Healy, "Good Science or Good Business?" *Hastings Center Report*, March/April 2000.

David Healy and David V. Sheehan, "Have Drug Companies Hyped Social Anxiety Disorder to Increase Sales? (Point-Counterpoint)," *Western Journal of Medicine*, December 2001.

Arianna Huffington, "Peppermint Prozac," *U.S. News & World Report*, August 18–25, 1997.

Walter Kirn, "The Danger of Suppressing Sadness: What If Holden Caulfield Had Been Taking Prozac?" *Time*, May 31, 1999.

————, "Living the Pharmaceutical Life," *Time*, September 29, 1997.

Nathan S. Kline, "Antidepressants May Bring New Life to Your Life," *Vogue*, July 1975.

Michael D. Lemonick, "The Mood Molecule," *Time*, September 29, 1997.

Mental Health Weekly, "Antidepressants: Do They Deliver on Their Promise?" July 15, 2002.

————, "FDA Issues Advisory on Antidepressants/Suicidal Thoughts in Children," November 3, 2003.

Alfred Meyer, "Listening to Paxil," *Psychology Today*, July/August 1996.

Terence Monmaney, "Remedy's U.S. Sales Zoom, but Quality Control Lags," *Los Angeles Times*, August 31, 1998.

Thomas J. Moore, "Hard to Swallow," *Washingtonian*, December 1997.

Jodie Morse et al., "Escaping from the Darkness: Drugs Like Prozac, Paxil, and Luvox Can Work Wonders for Clinically Depressed Kids. But What About the Long-Term Consequences?" *Time*, May 31, 1999.

J. Madeleine Nash, "Nature's Prozac?" *Time*, September 22, 1997.

David Noonan, "Prozac vs. Placebos: A New Study Concludes That America's Favorite Antidepressants Are Little Better than Sugar Pills. Have the Drugs Been Overhyped? It's Not That Simple," *Newsweek*, July 15, 2002.

Sherwin B. Nuland, "The Pill of Pills," *New York Review of Books*, June 9, 1994.

Kelly Patricia O'Meara, "Will British Ban Spur FDA to Act?" *Insight on the News*, February 17, 2004.

Claudia Rowe, "Women and Depression: Are We Being Overdosed?" *Redbook*, March 1992.

Melanie Scheller, "The Brave New World of Antidepressants," *Current Health 2*, January 1997.

Carla Spartos, "Sarafem Nation," *Village Voice*, December 12, 2000.

Marcello Spinella, "Psychoactive Herbal Medications," *Skeptical Inquirer*, January 2001.

Time, "Drug of the Year?" December 16, 1957.

Shankar Vedantam, "Antidepressant Makers Withhold Data on Children," *Washington Post*, January 29, 2004.

Anthony Wolff, "Medicine for Melancholy," *Saturday Review*, February 21, 1976.

Robert Wright, "The Coverage of Happiness: When Prozac Meets Universal Coverage," *New Republic*, March 14, 1994.

Web Sites

All About Depression, www.allaboutdepression.com. This Web site is operated by Prentiss Price, a counseling psychologist, with the goal of providing accurate, current, and relevant information about clinical depression for the general public. The site includes information about the types and uses of antidepressants.

Briefing on Drugs for Depression, http://thomasjmoore.com/pages/depress.shtml. This Web site operated by investigative journalist Thomas J. Moore features articles and information that argue that antidepressants have serious side effects and little benefit.

DepressionRemedy.com, www.depressionremedy.com. This site is owned and operated by Natural Pharmacy, a company that researches and sells herbal and natural remedies for various ailments. It includes information on the illness of depression and on natural products, including St. John's wort, ginkgo biloba, and ginseng.

JusticeSeekers.com, www.justiceseekers.com. This Web site is maintained by a group of trial lawyers who have brought wrongful death lawsuits against antidepressant manufacturers. It includes information on various lawsuits in which antidepressants are blamed for violent acts and suicide.

Learn About Paxil, www.paxil.com. A Web site operated by GlaxoSmithKline, the manufacturer of the antidepressant Paxil (paroxetine). It includes information on Paxil and depression and features self-tests on anxiety disorders and related conditions.

Prozac.com, www.prozac.com. This site operated by Eli Lilly and Company, the manufacturer of Prozac, includes information on the antidepressant and includes a self-assessment depression test.

Zoloft.com, www.zoloft.com. This Web site is operated by Pfizer, the manufacturer of the popular antidepressant Zoloft (sertraline). It features information on the drug and on depression and other mental health disorders.

INDEX

Abramowitz, Jonathan, 161
acetylcholine, 43
Advertising Age (journal), 159
Affective Spectrum Disorder (ASD), 60
akathisia, 136–37
alcohol, 22, 23, 51
Alemaeon of Croton, 22
alkaloids, psychotropic, 22
Alpert, Jonathan, 149, 150
American Journal of Psychiatry, 97, 139
American Psychiatric Association, 75, 76, 160
amines, biogenic, 125
anorexia, 79
antidepressants
  annual sales of, 19
  can cause violent behavior, 133–41
  first modern, discovery and development of, 25–30
  may cause teen suicide, 142–47
  reason for slowness to catch on, 36–41
  research on next wave of, 166–68
Antidepressant Sourcebook, The (Morrison), 25
antihistamines, 42–43
Aprepitant, 167–68
Arabic medicine, 23
Asclepiades, 22
Assyrian Herbal, 22
Atropa belladonna, 22
Avicenna, 23
Ayd, Frank J., 37

barbiturates, 24
Barondes, Samuel H., 110
Bell, George S., 77
benzodiazepines, 53–56
  addictive nature of, 55
  see also Librium; Valium
Berger, Frank, 52
Berle, Milton, 53
Beyond Prozac (Norden), 118
Blackwell, Barry, 44

Bloomfield, Harold H., 127
Bosworth, David, 34
brain
  changes in, from Prozac, 113–14
  effects of serotonin on, 100–101
  stress hormones and, 167
Brand, Barry, 159
Brandes, Lorne, 122
Braun, Stephen, 63
Breggin, Peter R., 63–65, 137
Bridges, Patrick, 131
Brodie, Bernard, 57
Brown, Richard, 124

Carlsson, Arvid, 57
Cass, Hyla, 126
catecholamine, 28–29, 30
Celexa, 143
  effects of, in children, 144
  see also selective serotonin reuptake inhibitors
children
  effects of SSRIs in, 144
  FDA on use of antidepressants in, 142
  use of Prozac in, 78–79, 142
  prevalence of, 145
  risk of suicide from, 146–47
chloral hydrate, 24
chlorpromazine, 114
Church of Scientology, 94
Citizen Commission on Human Rights (CCHR), 94
Cobb, Nathan, 103
cognitive behavioral therapy, 161
Cohen, Irvin, 53
Cole, Jonathan O., 40
Cooley, Donald G., 31
Coppen, Alec, 57, 58
Cornwell, John, 121
corticotropin-releasing hormone (CRH), 168
Cowdry, Rex, 157
Crane, George E., 33

Darkness Visible (Styron), 13

Davidson, Jonathan, 130, 131
deadly nightshade, 22
Dempsay, Daryl, 136
depression
  benefits of, 150–51
  clinical definition of, 13–14
  diagnosis of, 75–76
  new research in biology of, 167
  prevalence of, 14, 37
  psychostimulants in treatment of,
    153
  severe, St. John's wort is not
    effective in, 129–32
  symptoms of, 85, 124–25
  treatment for, history of, 14–16,
    21–24
  views on, in 1960s, 38–39
depressive disorder (clinical
    depression), 13
Desyrel (trazodone), 48–49
*Diagnostic and Statistical Manual of
  Mental Disorders* (American
  Psychiatric Association), 75, 76
Dick, Philip K., 166
Diller, Lawrence, 145
Do Androids Dream of Electric Sleep?
  (Dick), 166
Douglas, Joel, 135
drug studies
  FDA approval of drugs and, 15–16
  Prozac, manipulation of data
    from, 63–68
Dunner, David, 149, 150, 153, 154
dysthymic disorder/dysthymia, 14,
  75–76

Eber Papyrus, 22
Ecstasy (MDMA), 101
Elavil (amitriptyline), 17, 45
  see also tricyclic antidepressants
electroconvulsive therapy, 37–38,
  39
Elias, Marilyn, 142
Eli Lilly and Company
  lawsuits against, 84, 90, 138
  Prozac marketing by, 72
    for women, 162–65
  research on Prozac by, 58
    criticism of, 64–68
Elliott, Carl, 157

Equanil (meprobamate), 53

Faldt, Erica, 106–107
Fassler, David, 145
Feighner, John, 59
Fenfluramine, 101
Finz, Leonard, 91, 93
5-HTP (5-hydroxytryptophan), 125,
  126, 127
Fleming, Alexander, 26
fluoxetine. *See* Prozac
Food and Drug Administration
  (FDA), 15
  approval of Prozac by, 59, 116
    criticism of, 63–68
    link with suicide and, 99–100
  regulation of drug advertising by,
    164
  on use of antidepressants in
    children, 142
Freud, Sigmund, 16, 112, 113
Fuller, Ray, 58, 87

Gaddum, John, 56–57
Galen, 22
Gersten, Michelle, 79
ginkgo biloba, 15, 124, 127, 128
Goldschmidt, Debra, 129
Gorman, Jack, 92, 93, 98, 101
Grady, Denise, 90
Greenspan, Miriam, 150
Griesinger, Wilhelm, 24

Hadley, Joshua, 47
Hala, Rhonda, 90–91
Hapworth, William, 80
Harris, Eric, 140
Hartman, Brynn, 133, 134, 140
Hartman, Phil, 133, 134
Healing Anxiety with Herbs
  (Bloomfield), 127
Healing Through the Dark
  (Greenspan), 151
Healy, David, 56
Hellerstein, David, 73, 76, 78
Hemlock, Camille, 75
Herman, John, 152
hippocampus, 167
Hippocrates, 22
History of Psychiatry, A (Shorter), 51

Hoffman, Joel S., 77
hyoscyamine, 22

imipramine (Tofranil), 17, 25, 29, 114
  action of, 111
  development of, 26–27
  as "dirty" drug, 45
  reliability of, 29
  side effects of, 43, 47
  see also tricyclic antidepressants
iproniazid, 16
  development of, 26, 29, 31–35
Isaly, Samuel D., 70

*Journal of the American Medical
  Association*, 130

Katz, Russell, 143, 147
kava kava, 127, 128
Kinkle, Kip, 140
Kline, Nathan S., 32, 33, 39
Kopit Cohen, Sandra, 72, 76
Kramer, Peter D., 42, 103, 108, 112
Kuhn, Ronald, 42

Lane, Roger, 136
Leary, Timothy, 108
Leber, Paul, 100
Levin, Andrew, 72, 78
Lewis-Hall, Freda, 122
Librium (chlordiazepoxide), 38, 54
Liebowitz, Michael R., 80
Listening to Prozac (Kramer), 42,
  103, 108, 112, 163
Loomer, Harry P., 32
Lowney, Michael, 106
L-phenylalanine, 126, 127
L-tryptophan, 126, 127
L-tyrosine, 126, 127
Ludwig, Bernie, 52
Luther, Martin, 14

Magowan, Margot, 162
MAOIs. *See* monoamine oxidase
  inhibitors
Marano, Hara, 148
March, John, 145
marketing
  of Paxil as cure for shyness,
    155–59

  ethics of, 159–61
  of Prozac, 72
  to women, 162–65
Marsilid. *See* iproniazid
Medawar, Charles, 36
melancholia, 14
melatonin, 126
Merital, 72
Miller, Mark, 146
Miller, Matthew, 135–36, 146
Miller, Michael C., 166
Miltown (meprobamate), 52–53
Molloy, Bryan, 87, 88, 89
monoamine oxidase, 30, 43
monoamine oxidase inhibitors
  (MAOIs), 16, 25, 30, 79, 94, 96
  action of, 125
  Prozac compared to, 73–74
  side effects of, 17, 38, 43–45
Morrison, Andrew L., 25

National Institute of Mental Health
  on prevalence of depression, 14,
    92, 131
  on prevalence of social anxiety
    disorder, 160
  on symptoms of depression,
    124–25
National Institutes of Health, 57
  analysis of antidepressant studies
    by, 40
nerve chemistry, 27–28
Neuropeptide Y, 168
neurotransmitters, 27
  amino acids as, 126
  effects of antidepressants on, 17
Newsweek (magazine), 61
Newton, Jeff, 137
New York Times (newspaper), 61
nicotine addiction, 80
Nierenberg, Andrew, 151
Norden, Michael, 118, 121–22
norepinephrine, 17, 45, 125
Norpramin (desipramine), 45, 46

opium, 21–22, 23, 51–52
opium poppy (*Papaver somniferum*),
  21

panic disorders, 80

Paracelsus, 23
paraldehyde, 24
Paris, Peter, 109
Parker, Jerrold S., 91
Paxil (paroxetine), 116, 120
  effects of, in children, 144
  marketing of, as cure for shyness,
    155–59
    ethics of, 159–61
  side effects of, 125
  weight gain and, 152
  see also selective serotonin
    reuptake inhibitors
Payk, T.R., 21
Pearce, John, 105
People (magazine), 134
Perelman, S.J., 53
Peselow, Eric, 119
Peters, Al, 105
pharmacotherapy
  in ancient world, 21–22
  in Middle Ages, 22–23
  nineteenth-century advances in,
    23–24
  see also psychopharmacology
phytomedicines, 127–28
phytotherapeutic polypragmasy, 22
Pomme, Pierre, 14
Pope, Harrison, 60
Power to Harm, The (Cornwell), 121
Premenstrual Dysphoric Disorder
  (PMDD), 162–63
Prien, Robert F., 75–76
Provigil, 153
Prozac (fluoxetine), 17–19, 43
  accounts of negative experience
    with, 95, 104–105
  accounts of success with, 60–62,
    69–71, 74–75, 81–89
  backlash against, 90–102
  criticism of FDA testing of, 63–68
  development of, 56–58
  has changed practice of
    psychiatry, 110–15
  ignorance about action of,
    100–101, 107
  link with suicidal behavior and,
    97–100
  possible long-term risks of, 80,
    122

sales of, 84, 92, 106, 117
side effects of, 76–77, 96, 120,
  125–26
use of, in children, 78–79, 142
  effects of, 144
  prevalence of, 145
use of, in nondepressive
  disorders, 66, 80, 92, 105, 112,
  117
weight loss and, 79–80
see also selective serotonin
  reuptake inhibitors
Prozac Nation (Wurtzel), 164
psychiatry
  impact of benzodiazepines on, 55
  Prozac/SSRIs have changed
    practice of, 110–15
psychoactive drugs, 51–52
psychological therapies
  in ancient world, 22, 25–26
  cognitive behavioral therapy, 161
psychopharmacology
  cosmetic, 52, 108
  modern, birth of, 110
psychostimulants, 153
Pure Food and Drug Act (1906), 15

receptors, 27–28
  serotonin, 113
Recognizing the Depressed Patient
  (Ayd), 37
Reil, Johann Christian, 24
reserpine, 26, 28
Rhazes, 23
Road to Miltown, The (Perelman), 53
Roose, Steven, 72, 73
Rorie, Somlynn, 124
Rosenbaum, Jerrold, 94, 99, 153
Ross, Jerilyn, 158

SAM-e, 124, 126, 127
Saunders, John C., 32
Scherbel, Arthur L., 34
schizophrenia, 16, 25
Schumer, Fran, 69
Science of Happiness, The (Braun), 63
scopolamine, 22
selective serotonin reuptake
  inhibitors (SSRIs), 18, 59
  action of, 125

can cause violent behavior,
133–41
effects of, in children, 144
have changed practice of
psychiatry, 110–15
possible long-term risks of, 122
side effects of, 150–53
use of, in disorders other than
depression, 150
Serafem, 162
see also Prozac
serotonin, 17, 45, 83, 125
discovery of, 28
disorders associated with, 46
effects of, on brain, 100–101
receptors for, 113
role of, 56–57
see also selective serotonin
reuptake inhibitors
Serzone, 121
Severinghaus, Elmer L., 31
Shorter, Edward, 18, 51
Should I Medicate My Child? (Diller),
145
side effects
of imipramine, 43, 47
of monoamine oxidase inhibitors,
17, 43–45
of Prozac, 76–77, 96, 120
of selective serotonin reuptake
inhibitors, 150–53
of tricyclic antidepressants, 17,
45–46
social anxiety disorder, 151, 155–56
marketing of Paxil as cure for,
156–59
ethics of, 159–60
prevalence of, 160
Sorosky, Arthur, 135
SSRIs. *See* selective serotonin
reuptake inhibitors
St. John's wort, 15, 19, 23, 124,
127, 128
comparison with synthetic
antidepressants, 126
dangers of, 131
is not effective in severe
depression, 129–32
sales of, 132
Stein, Murray, 157, 158

stimulants, Prozac compared with,
65
Styron, William, 13
Substance P, 167–68
suicide/suicidal behavior
akathisia and, 136–37
SSRIs are associated with, 90,
135–36
studies showing Prozac's link
with, 97–99
FDA's response to, 99–100
in teens, antidepressants may
cause, 142–47
Sussman, Norman, 94, 96, 97
synapses, 27

teen suicide, antidepressants may
cause, 142–47
Teicher, Martin, 97, 101
Thompson, Tracy, 83
Thorazine, 27, 29
Time (magazine), 60
Tofranil. *See* imipramine
Tollefson, Gary, 104
Torello, Celeste, 137
tricyclic antidepressants, 16, 25,
29–30, 94, 95
gender difference in response to,
118
Prozac compared to, 73–74
side effects of, 17, 45–46

Valium (diazepam), 38, 53–55
vapours, 14–15
vasopressin, 168
Vedantam, Shankar, 155
Vickery, Andy, 138

Wallace, Asha, 106
Walton, Sherri, 146
Wartik, Nancy, 116
Waters, Rob, 133
Wellbutrin, 121
Wesbecker, Joseph, 139
Williamson, Patricia, 136
Windsor, Lindsay, 95
Winters, Judith, 104–105
women
repackaging of Prozac for, 162–65
use of Prozac by, 117

Wong, David, 87, 88
World Health Organization, on
prevalence of depression, 37
Wurtzel, Elizabeth, 163–64

Xanax, 72, 90

Zelmid (zimelidine), 57–58
Zisook, Sidney, 119, 121

Zito, Julie Magno, 145
Zoloft (sertraline), 116, 120, 143
can cause violent behavior,
133–41
as control in studies of St. John's
wort, 130, 132
effects of, in children, 144
see also selective serotonin
reuptake inhibitors